"Jeff Iorg has made an enormous contribution to the critical area of ministry and leadership. It isn't what a minister does so much as what he is that makes him effective. This is a must-read for every minister who strives for excellence in ministry. I recommend it without reservation."

James T. Draper Jr.
President Emeritus
LifeWay Christian Resources

"As I was reading Dr. Iorg's book, I kept thinking, *This man has walked in my shoes!* His counsel is biblical. His applications are practical. Every seminarian, pastor, and church or Christian organization staff member should make it a must-read. It has been said that reputation is precious, but character is priceless. This good book, written with the honesty and transparency of the author, underscores that reality."

Jim Henry
Pastor Emeritus
First Baptist Church Orlando

"In his book, *The Character of Leadership,* Jeff Iorg defines lasting leadership as character, not capacity or competency. The making of a great leader is built on what God intends you to *be* rather than doing the leading God intends for you to *do.* His purpose is first and foremost to shape you into the image of

Jesus, the greatest leader of all time. You can *be* the leader God called you to *be!*"

Rick Warren
Pastor, Saddleback Church
Author, Purpose-Driven Life

"Jeff Iorg is eminently qualified to write this volume on leadership because he possesses and has consistently demonstrated the qualities of leadership described in this book. These qualities have graced his life as a pastor, church planter, state convention executive, and now as president of Golden Gate Baptist Theological Seminary. This book should be required reading for every minister of the gospel. The chapter on integrity and the no-nonsense chapter on purity are very much needed in our times and worth the price of the book and the investment of your time to read it. Even the seasoned leader will be enriched by the wisdom of the author."

J. Robert White
Executive Director
Georgia Baptist Convention

THE CHARACTER OF
LEADERSHIP

Kerrie - Ann -
Thanks for your
service !

THE CHARACTER OF
LEADERSHIP

Nine Qualities that Define Great Leaders

JEFF IORG

B&H
PUBLISHING GROUP
Nashville, Tennessee

ISBN: 978-0-8054-4532-9

Published by B & H Publishing Group,
Nashville, Tennessee

Dewey Decimal Classification: 303.3
Subject Heading: CHARACTER \ LEADERSHIP
CHRISTIAN LIFE

8 9 10 11 12   16 15 14 13 12

Contents

1. The Quest for Character   1

2. Maintaining Integrity   23

3. Finding Security   47

4. Maintaining Purity   70

5. Learning Humility   93

6. Developing Servanthood   115

7. Gaining Wisdom   138

8. Practicing Discipline   160

9. Showing Courage   182

10. Sustaining Passion   204

11. Continuing the Quest for Character   226

CHAPTER ONE

The Quest
for Character

IN MY TWENTIES, I was determined to change the world. In my thirties, I tried to reform the church. In my early forties, I discovered I was the problem.

That was a difficult day.

Like most young leaders, my early ministry was marked by a passion to change something. My decision to change the world obviously didn't work. Then I decided the church was the problem. So I started a new one. While it grew into a strong healthy church, something still was not right. No matter how hard I tried to restructure the people and circumstances around me, I still was deeply frustrated.

Through a painful series of circumstances, some of which you will read about in this book, God brought me face to face with this hard reality—my problem was me! So, for the past decade my focus has been on *becoming* the leader God intends me to be rather than *doing* the leading God intends me to do.

Don't misunderstand—I am very busy doing! I am committed to energetically applying myself to the work God assigns me. People who evaluate me give me high marks for industry, dependability, and attention to duty. Finding enough to do is not and never has been my problem.

If you read anything in this book that leads you to shirk your responsibilities, delve into some ethereal justification for ineffectiveness, or drift toward laziness in ministry, then you are misreading me. God wants you to work hard and to study how to improve your skills so you work more effectively. Other books, other very important books, will help you do that. Most schools, seminaries, and seminars focus on these skills. Many of them are helpful. But this book is not about how to *do* leadership. It is about how to *be* a leader.

The reality is too many young leaders start out like me. They believe if they learn enough facts and accomplish enough tasks, they will not only satisfy God, their followers, and their peers—they will also find deep fulfillment. I no longer believe that. Now I know that deep fulfillment comes from knowing God intimately, understanding his purpose to shape me into the image of Jesus Christ, and discerning how he is using his Word and my circumstances to shape me toward that purpose.

Becoming the Leader
God Intends You to Be

God Has a Clear Purpose for You!

God has an ultimate purpose for you. Simply put, he wants to shape your character to make you like Jesus Christ. Romans 8:28–29 summarizes this purpose: "We know that all things work together for the good of those who love God: those who are called according to His purpose. For those He foreknew He also predestined to be conformed to the image of His Son."

These verses are packed with meaning! While volumes have been written about them, let's summarize the key points as they relate to character development.

God has a definite purpose. That is clear in these verses. We are called "according to His purpose"; therefore, God must have one. God is doing something specific in each one of us.

God's purpose is to conform us to the image of Jesus. This is also very clear. We are to be "conformed to the image of His Son." God is busy remaking his children, including all of us leaders. He is busy making us more and more like Jesus.

God is intentional about his purpose. Romans uses strong theological language—"those He foreknew He also predestined." God knows and determines, in ways we can never understand, that we *will* be conformed to the image of Jesus. God is relentless in this endeavor. He wills it—and what God wills, he accomplishes. Long ago, God reminded Isaiah, "I am God, and there is none like me. I make known the end from the beginning, from ancient times, what is still to come. I say: *My purpose will stand, and I will do all that I please*" (Isa. 46:9b–10 NIV). We need that same reminder. God is intentional and purposeful in conforming us to the image of Jesus.

God's ultimate purpose gives meaning to our circumstances. Usually, the "all things" in these verses is applied when bad things happen. Comfort is drawn from these verses during crisis, bereavement, or tragedy. That certainly is appropriate. But the phrase "all things" means that all circumstances of life, bad and *good*, transpire and conspire to change us. God is at work through all our circumstances to shape us into the image of Jesus. Accepting and affirming that one great spiritual reality causes our circumstances, no matter how puzzling, to make sense in the context of Christian character development.

God's purpose is good. God allows circumstances that have good *results* in our lives. Not every circumstance is good—the death of a child, a tragic illness, a national calamity, or other horrific events cannot be called good. God does not call them good.

Only fake piety or some form of spiritual denial leads to calling these events good. But God promises good can come from every circumstance as its meaning is related to his ultimate purpose. God can bring a good result, inner conformation to Jesus, from whatever he allows us to experience.

Now make it more personal. God has a purpose for you. His purpose is to make you more and more like Jesus. He is relentless in his quest. God will organize and orchestrate circumstances to accomplish his purpose—so there is purpose in your experiences as a leader. God's purpose for you—shaping you in the image of Jesus—is good and will always be good for you. And that is very good news!

Leadership as a Laboratory

Have you ever wondered why God places people in certain leadership roles, positions, or responsibilities? The usual answer for most leaders is "because God wants to use me to (fill in the blank)." That was certainly my perspective earlier in ministry. I thought God wanted me to be a pastor so I could lead a church, teach people the Bible, reach people with the gospel, strengthen families, and impact our community. Later, I thought God wanted me to be a church planter so I could connect with lost people, demonstrate a new model of church, and create some new paradigms of ministry.

When God called me to be a denominational executive, I thought it was to bring fresh vision to a convention of churches, create new ways of thinking
about cooperative ministry, and find new ways to
encourage and nurture leaders.

All of those were good reasons why God placed
me in certain roles over the years. But none of them
were the ultimate reason. The ultimate reason God
assigned me to any position was because he could
best use that position, at that time, to accomplish
his purpose of shaping me into the image of Jesus.

This understanding first dawned on me as I
considered leaving the pastorate of the church I
planted to become a denominational executive. As
I meditated on that change process, there was one
reality I did fully understand and was reluctant to
admit. The reality was, as a pastor, I was coasting.

By coasting, I mean the daily spiritual challenge
of doing my job was not compelling. Our church
was healthy, I basically knew what to do to keep
it that way, and I was enjoying the ride! Changing
ministry roles, changing to a kind of ministry in
which I had little experience or expertise, and changing leadership identities was a staggering thought.
As I prayed, asking the Father why he wanted such
a change, this idea emerged. God wanted me in a
laboratory where I was once again on the growing
edge, desperate to know him and to become more
like Jesus.

For me, my pastorate had become like swimming laps. I was stroking along, doing well, staying in shape, keeping things moving, and making steady progress. Answering God's call to this new position was like being tossed overboard into the ocean. No more gliding along! Once again, I would be swimming for my spiritual life.

By the time I was asked to consider becoming a seminary president, these convictions had formed more fully. When the search committee contacted me, my first prayer was "Father, is this the place you want me to be so you can make me more like Jesus?" Reflecting on almost ten years as an executive leader, I sensed some of the same feelings I had when I left the pastorate. I was more honest with myself, with my wife, and with God in answering his call this time.

I do not believe God has primarily called me to be a seminary president because of what I can do for the seminary. I believe God has placed me here because of how he will use these circumstances to shape me in ever-fresh, ever-deeper ways to be like Jesus. Part of that process, obviously, is serving and leading the seminary—doing my job! But I am much more eager to discover what the seminary community, challenges, and circumstances will do *in me* than what I will do for them.

Leadership roles, positions, callings, or assignments are God's laboratories for leaders. God places us where we are (or may call us to a new place) so he can have the perfect laboratory for continuing to change us into the image of Jesus. God has control of our circumstances and will use them to shape us—if we learn to discern his work and allow him to do it.

The rest of this book is about how God accomplishes this process.

Character Building 101

Some legitimate questions to ask at this point are, "Does character really continue to develop over a lifetime? After all, aren't we shaped as young children into who we are? Aren't the 'formative years' of our youth really when we finalize our inner core? Do we really change much after that?"

Certainly, personality and values are profoundly shaped by genetics, childhood experiences, family relationships, and other early life influences. But are these really the final, formative processes for a Christian? The answer is clearly no.

The Christian doctrine of sanctification—the biblical process of growing in grace, of becoming a fully devoted disciple of Jesus, of continually learning the ways of God—clearly calls for lifelong character development. While personality is largely determined by genetics and early environmental factors, character continues to be shaped and developed over a lifetime.

How then, does God shape character? God shapes character by bringing together three converging streams that flow toward his purpose—the Bible, circumstances, and disciplined discernment of his purposes.

God Uses the Bible

The most significant source for character development is the Bible. God's Word is the standard by which all of your impressions, thoughts, feelings, perceptions, choices, and values must be measured. Reading the Bible regularly (with a goal of daily), studying the Bible carefully, hearing the Bible preached and taught clearly, and memorizing key passages of Scripture are foundational to Christian character development. Making the Bible the center of your values and choices keeps this entire process from becoming an emotional, subjective experience.

This cannot be emphasized enough. In a postmodern world, pop psychology and pop religion focus on the endless search for inner peace, inner fulfillment, and inner actualization through all kinds of self-defined, self-motivated processes of self-realization. That's too much self! The urgency of this quest, and the fact that so many people are on it, speaks of our intuitive need to grow inwardly. But sadly, leaving God's Word out of the equation has perverted this God-created desire.

Unfortunately, postmodern spiritual seekers often develop a pseudo-intellectual, pseudo-spiritual mind-set void of any submission to absolute Truth or ultimate accountability. They want to develop their inner person but on their own terms. This is why it is essential to regularly engage God's Word. Read it, memorize it, meditate on it, study it, and most of all, let it control your decisions and attitudes. Without the Bible as a guide, you will be lost in a sea of subjective spiritual experiences.

The desire to become more like Jesus is evidence of a healthy Christian commitment. You are seeking God's ultimate purpose and expect to be changed. For this process to genuinely result in Christ being formed in you, however, the Bible must be a vital part of your life. You must submit this entire process of character development to the Word of God and what it teaches about life, about God, and about experiencing God.

God Uses Your Circumstances

The second significant instrument God uses is your life circumstances. While God uses all circumstances, particularly for leaders God uses the place you are serving. God uses the difficulties of your ministry setting—and all places have something that makes them difficult. He also uses the people he has allowed in your life, both friends and foes. God uses all the events, conditions, and relationships you encounter as a leader to shape you. This also includes the positive circumstances—the opportunities he provides for success and progress. God uses circumstances, events you have little or no control over, to do his work in you.

Joseph, the Old Testament leader (Gen. 37–50), had a life filled with unusual circumstances he did not cause and could not control. He came from a large family so dysfunctional his brothers sold him into slavery. Joseph lived in a foreign country, rising from slavery to a significant leadership role only to be imprisoned for a crime he did not commit. After several years in prison, he was returned to a prominent leadership role in Egypt. This position made him instrumental in feeding Egypt and able to provide for other nations during a severe famine.

Desperately hungry, Joseph's brothers came to Egypt to buy food. Because Joseph's appearance had changed over the years and his brothers assumed he was dead, they did not recognize him. He sold them grain, conspired to have them go home, and then return with their youngest brother, father, and families. Finally, Joseph revealed himself to them. Panic-stricken, they assumed they would be punished or killed for selling Joseph into slavery.

Joseph responded to his brothers' fear with one of the most remarkable affirmations in the Bible. Joseph said, "You planned evil against me; God planned it for good to bring about the present result—the survival of many people" (Gen. 50:20). Another translation (NIV) reads, "You intended to harm me, but God intended it for good." Could you say that to people who sold you into slavery, condemned you to a life apart from your family, and were the reason you went to prison? Doubtful, unless you shared Joseph's deep conviction that God supervises your circumstances. This deep conviction—that God supervises your circumstances and will accomplish good through them—can be called "the Joseph principle."

Not only does God use circumstances you cannot control; he also uses circumstances you create or control for the specific purpose of developing character. You can intentionally create procedures and practices for yourself to promote your own character development. You may wonder if that really works, if your character can continually be developed through shaping your external realities.

The answer is a resounding yes! One clear example clinches the case: parenting. God uses parents to shape their children's character through controlling their circumstances. Parents create procedures and practices to help their children develop honesty, generosity, gratitude, work ethic, and other desirable character qualities.

For example, we frequently refuse to give our children money but enable them to earn it. We are not being selfish. We are simply structuring circumstances to teach resourcefulness, give our children a sense of responsibility, and deepen their appreciation for the value of money. Parenting is continually structuring circumstances to shape character.

What works for children, at least in principle, also works for adults. Without parents monitoring your behavior, however, you must structure your own circumstances to shape your character. As leaders, we must have the discipline to do it for ourselves. We structure circumstances we can control and then allow them to shape our character. Setting up learning opportunities, creating structure or standards to control our behavior, and becoming accountable to others are not "mind games" to fool us into acting differently. These are valid strategies for shaping character over a lifetime. Throughout this book, examples of these kinds of self-initiated structures will be described as a primary means God can use to shape your character.

God uses his Word and circumstances, both those you control and those you do not, to mold your character. God's Word and your circumstances converge to reveal new insights into your spiritual growth. To fully discover those insights requires development of an additional, important spiritual skill—disciplined discernment.

Disciplined Discernment

Joseph was able to affirm the good God did through his circumstances because he had proper perspective. This kind of mature perspective, living out the Joseph principle, comes from *asking God the right question* and *allowing time to discover God's answer.* Working through this process—asking the right question and allowing time to discover the answer is called disciplined discernment.

What is the right question? The right question to ask about your circumstances is "Father, why are you allowing this to happen to me?" The attitude and emphasis is key to asking the question appropriately. Your attitude must reflect submission to God's purposes, respect for his wisdom, and an expectation of a positive outcome. You are not accusing God with the question but simply asking him to reveal how the current circumstance relates to his purpose of shaping you into the image of Jesus.

The emphasis in the question is not on "why" but on "this." Do not ask *"Why me?"* Instead, ask "Father, why *this?"* Sometimes, our concern with "why" something happens is based on a subtle arrogance. Deep down, we believe we do not deserve this kind of treatment! Be more concerned with "this." Ask God to show you some specific connection of your current circumstances to the purpose of Jesus' image being shaped in you.

The second part of disciplined discernment is allowing enough time to pass to discover the answer. Sometimes, the process is intense and the answer comes quickly. Other times, the process is more complex and the answers take years to discover. Sometimes, when circumstances remain the same over an extended period of time, the full answer might take decades to unfold in your understanding.

For example, my first pastorate was very challenging. The church was really good to me—supporting me as I developed preaching and pastoral skills, paying for me to attend seminary, and tolerating my learning leadership skills at their expense. While they treated me kindly, and I have come to appreciate them more and more over the years, it was still a difficult church because of the diversity of the membership.

The church had people from almost every walk of life. There were union workers and managers. We had a prosecutor and people he had put in jail. The people had very diverse educational levels, social backgrounds, and church traditions. Rich people sat next to the very poor. Well-educated served with the functionally illiterate. About every sin imaginable had been committed by someone in that church and all too frequently involving others in the church!

I often wondered why God allowed my first church to be so challenging. Several years passed before I learned the answer. God used that church to teach me how to work with people from many backgrounds. When I left pastoral ministry and became a denominational executive working with several hundred churches, the skills I learned in that first church were skills I used daily. Who could have imagined? God was changing me and shaping me for future challenges. It took almost a decade to understand why God had allowed me to have such a difficult first pastorate.

More personally, during my early years in ministry I had several very intense critics. Like pugnacious bulldogs, they consistently pointed out my flaws—often verbally and sometimes in writing! More than one of them left me in tears, wondering if the ministry was really worth doing. The sharpness and frequency of those attacks was incredibly painful. One morning, while praying about (and against!) my critics, I finally asked the "why" question with the right attitude and emphasis. As an answer, God turned on a movie projector in my mind and reminded me of repeated incidents where I had verbally attacked others.

That was not a fun morning at the movies! My memory flooded with specific times I had harshly criticized others. One incident was particularly hypocritical and painful. Reliving it, from the perspective of the person I had attacked, was devastating. I realized that my sharp tongue, quick wit, and hostile humor had harmed many people. I also realized why God had allowed others to attack me. God was determined to spotlight this flaw in my character and allow pain to motivate me to change. Because of this experience, I became much more patient with people.

This spiritual confrontation created a significant desire for me to change the way I use words in relationships. This is a watershed issue for me and one I have worked hard to change. Much to my surprise, several years later during an annual review, my evaluators said I am sometimes "too nice." While I have grown significantly, I doubt that was true!

God is committed to shaping you into the image of Jesus. He uses his Word to set the standard and allows circumstances to turn up the heat. Discernment, asking the right question and allowing enough time to pass for perspective to reveal God's purpose, is essential to understanding what God is doing in your leadership laboratory.

The Dark Side of Character Development

Ministry leaders are unique because character defines their qualification to lead. The biblical qualifications for leadership stress character more than skill, education, or experience. Conversely, for ministry leaders, character failure undermines and cancels out prior results to a greater degree than for leaders in other fields. Character failure for ministers often invalidates everything done prior to the sin. Churches are devastated, people leave wounded and discouraged, and ministries take a long time to recover (if they ever do).

Character flaws or failures in other fields (like among business, military, and political leaders) are not usually as devastating. Public opinion often forgives those leaders, excusing their actions in amazing ways! President Clinton's sexual behavior and his remarkable popularity after leaving office is one example of this.

Accepting the high calling of ministry leadership is accepting this greater weight of responsibility. You can't shirk it. You won't be the exception to this rule. You won't be able to go quietly. If your character flaws (and all of us have them) turn into character failures, the breach of trust with your followers will have devastating consequences.

Let your mind's eye imagine the faces of the people you lead. They are counting on you, not just for what you do for them but for the Christian character you develop and demonstrate to them. They may not articulate this often or clearly, but the primary issue for them is trust. Can you be trusted with the secret things of their lives? Can they be spiritually vulnerable with you? Can they trust you enough to let you speak truth to them?

Character collapse by Christian leaders breaks trust with Christian followers. That is its most devastating result. Followers close themselves to further spiritual direction and lose the opportunity to receive the ministry God could provide through subsequent leaders.

Every leader must make a determined commitment to avoid this tragic outcome! But more than that, as leaders we must cooperate with God as he shapes the character of Christ in us. That result must become our passion!

Why These Character Qualities?

The list of character qualities included in this book is subjective. So how were they chosen? First, they come from personal experience. As God has shaped me, I have written and reflected on the process and progress. Some of these qualities have been and are core issues for me. Several are continuing areas of profound struggle and growth.

Second, they come from observing other leaders. I have observed ministry leaders for three decades and trained ministry leaders for more than ten years. During that time, I have looked for common characteristics in both successful leaders and leaders who struggled or failed. Both groups reveal what is required for effective leadership over the long haul.

Third, these qualities emerge from teaching on character development and listening to the responses. God has used church members, colleagues, students, and friends over the years to challenge my ideas and make me think more practically about the process of character development. Some of my worst ideas are on the cutting room floor thanks to the eye-rolling responses from past hearers. You can be grateful for the editing their frank responses provided.

So, while these nine character qualities are a subjective list, they are not a random untested collection. They represent the core of what it means to be a leader. They are the heart, the core, the solid center that sustains a leader over a lifetime.

Transparency

This book contains a lot of my journey. God has been working to remake me into the image of Jesus Christ for more than thirty years. There was and is a lot of work to do! Many of the principles and experiences in this book have been learned the hard way. By sharing them, my goal is transparency, not elevating my experience as a foolproof model. Many of the personal illustrations in this book are of my failures. Much of my growth as a Christian leader has happened when God turned these negative experiences into good opportunities for growth.

Transparency is often scarce among Christian leaders. When they share personal illustrations, leaders often careen between two extremes: self-celebration or catharsis. Appropriate transparency reveals enough to be helpful, but avoids self-promotion. Transparency protects persons who might be harmed by exposing confidential information, yet uses real illustrations to help you see real-life applications. Transparency allows you to look through the window of someone's life and learn from what you see. Like many leaders, my life is often lived in public. Admitting that, and inviting you in for a closer look is what I have tried to do. Balancing all this is tough. I hope I have come reasonably close!

Most books are success stories. This book is a work-in-progress story. God *is* shaping you and me into the image of Jesus—no matter our age or life status. None of us can claim that this process is finished. Perhaps some part of my story will encourage you in fresh ways to become more like Jesus. And, maybe we will meet someday and discuss what else I have learned about how God shapes character in the leadership lab. This book will end with a comma, not a period. Fresh experience with God should produce fresh insight as he continues to shape Jesus in me in the years ahead.

The simple goal of becoming more like Jesus should be the ultimate goal of every leader. Leaders are usually remembered for who they were, not what they did. Instead of building monuments to our ingenuity, we should be focused on building lives worth remembering.

How will you be remembered? What will you be remembered for? Most significant leaders accomplish much. But what they are remembered for is their character. Think about what you have heard (or said) at memorial services for leaders. The tributes are about character. I have never once heard anyone praised for enlarging the budget, hiring more staff, building a building, or writing a book!

So, join me in the journey of becoming a leader who makes a long-term impact and leaves a positive leadership legacy. Join me in the challenge of becoming more like Jesus Christ—the model leader. Join me in *becoming* a leader, not just doing leadership stuff. Join me in the quest for character, the character of Jesus Christ formed in you. This is the essence of what it means to be a man or woman of God. This is the core of a real leader.

CHAPTER TWO

Maintaining Integrity

IN ALMOST EVERY profession there is a renewed call for integrity among leaders. A fresh call to lead with integrity is happening among leaders in law, medicine, business, education, politics, sports, and ministry. Everyone wants leaders with integrity, thinks it's important, and definitely wants it demonstrated toward them. But fewer and fewer leaders seem to value integrity, know what it is, how to develop it, maintain it personally, or demonstrate it professionally.

Some leaders have a view of integrity that is too simplistic. If they have not had an affair or stolen money, then they have integrity! Unfortunately, it's not that simple. Maintaining integrity means more than appropriate sexual and fiscal behavior. While those are important issues, integrity touches all areas of a leader's life.

Defining Integrity

The word *integrity* comes from the Latin word *integritas* — the root word for *integer*. The root word means "whole, complete, or undivided." An integer is a whole number, not a fraction. A proper understanding of integrity can be built on this math imagery. A person of integrity is a whole, complete, undivided person — not segmented or fractionalized. No double-dealing, no double standards, and no double meanings! A person is whole, complete, undivided in words and actions and standards.

This changes the focus from simply behaving properly in any single area to behaving consistently in all areas all the time. That is a tougher challenge! You have integrity when you are the same in every place, in every circumstance, with every group of people.

Dictionary definitions of *integrity*, like Webster's for example, support this same idea. Integrity is the "quality or state of being complete or undivided." Note the use of the same meaning as derived from the root word *integer*. A person of integrity is whole or complete. The best understanding of integrity is being unified. A person of integrity has integrated his or her standards, words, and actions into one. Integrity, then, is saying what you mean, meaning what you say, doing what you say, and meaning what you do!

Another part of the definition of integrity is "firm adherence to a code of moral or artistic values." This strikes at the more common understanding of integrity—coming up to a certain standard. For Christian leaders, this means coming up to God's standards of moral and ethical behavior. In short, you bring your behavior in line with God's Word.

Both Old and New Testament root words support these ideas. The Hebrew root word for integrity means "complete, whole, or perfect." This supports the first part of the modern definition. New Testament words related to integrity carry an ethical dimension—righteousness, holiness, and purity. These ideas round out the twofold perspective on the meaning of integrity—wholeness and holiness.

A simple definition of integrity, which combines these ideas, is "consistently applying biblical principles in character and action." Integrity occurs when you integrate your beliefs and actions with the standards of Scripture so there is consistency. You have integrity when you conform your beliefs and actions to what the Bible teaches. This is the essence of Christian integrity. You align your attitudes, words, and actions with biblical truth. You strive for a seamless meshing of these in all areas of life—home, work, school, everywhere—to be a leader with integrity.

Spiritual Foundations
for Developing Integrity

Christian leaders have a unique opportunity to develop integrity and a unique responsibility to demonstrate integrity. We have spiritual resources to guide us and strengthen us through the process. Just wanting to have integrity is not enough. Having integrity at any given point in time is not enough. *Maintaining* integrity over a lifetime of changing and challenging personal and ministry situations must be our goal.

Maintaining integrity is, fundamentally, a continual spiritual quest. Over the years, there have been three spiritual convictions that have helped me develop and maintain integrity. Like a three-legged stool, these three statements form a spiritual foundation for integrity.

1. I am in submission to Jesus as Lord (Phil. 2:5–11)

Jesus is Lord. There is no negotiating that indisputable fact. My choice is submission to him, recognizing his Lordship. We must resist "make him Lord" theology and terminology. He is Lord, Master, Supervisor whether we "make him Lord" or not. He is the One to whom we are accountable. My only choice is submission to or rebellion against him. This is foundational to integrity. I am not a law unto myself. I do not set the standards. I am not the final authority on my beliefs, attitudes, or actions. Someone else is and that Someone is Jesus.

Have you ever made a study of the Lordship of Jesus and applied it to yourself *personally?* It's easy to theorize about Jesus as Lord or preach on the need for others to submit to his Lordship. It's much more difficult to make it personal. While volumes have been written attempting to exhaustively explain the Lordship of Jesus, consider these five affirmations as a summary of what the Bible teaches about this important subject. These statements can form a foundation for your understanding and affirmation of Jesus as your Lord.

1. Jesus is Lord by God's authority.
    a. Matthew 28:18, Jesus claimed all authority had been given to him.
    b. Acts 2:36, Jesus received his authority from God.
    c. Philippians 2:5–9, Jesus received all authority because of his work on the cross.
2. Jesus is Lord because of his resurrection.
    a. Ephesians 1:20, Jesus' resurrection preceded God's work of exalting him as Lord.
    b. Revelation 1:18, Jesus' resurrection demonstrated his power over the ultimate enemy—death.

3. Jesus' Lordship over every area of life is demonstrated by his miracles.
    a. Matthew 8:26–27, Jesus has power over nature.
    b. Matthew 9:1–8, Jesus has power over disease.
    c. Mark 9:25–27, Jesus has power over demons.
    d. John 11:44, Jesus has power over death.
4. Jesus' Lordship is timeless.
    a. Colossians 1:16–17, Jesus has always been Lord.
    b. Ephesians 1:20–21, Jesus is Lord now.
    c. Ephesians 1:21, Jesus will always be Lord.
5. Jesus' Lordship encompasses everything and everyone.
    a. Colossians 1:18, Jesus has supremacy over everything.
    b. Philippians 2:10–11, Jesus has supremacy over everyone.

Affirming a sound theology of the Lordship of Jesus is not enough. You must personalize it. How do you do that? For me, the best way to personalize Jesus as Lord is to regularly pray four prayers that remind me of his Lordship. Each of these prayers emerged from a crisis experience or a time of intense spiritual confrontation for me. Each of them became important because of the circumstances in which they were first prayed. Since then, they have become a permanent part of my devotional life and spiritual formation.

Do not misunderstand. I do not pray these prayers rotely, routinely, or mindlessly. They are not some kind of mantra or chant. I do not pray them every day. But I do return to one or more of them often. They are centering prayers for me. They bring me back to the core reality—Jesus is my Lord!

My first prayer is "Lord, I am expendable. Another day or another decade of life, whatever pleases you." That prayer was first prayed at midnight on December 31, 1999 as the year 2000 dawned. I know, technically, the new millennium did not start that night. But the world celebrated anyway!

My family attended a major Christian event, YouthLink 2000, which connected multiple meeting sites across the United States electronically for a national, simultaneous celebration of the millennium. As midnight drew near, we were challenged to write a prayer that summarized our response to the Lord at that moment. Concerns about the uncertainty of the future, questions about making a significant impact with my life, and impressions that God had some big changes in store for me led me to pray like this: "I am expendable. I exist to be used by God, not to use God. I have no guarantee of another moment of life beyond what God sustains. Another day or decade, whatever pleases

the Lord, is the span of my life." Praying this way
reminded me who is Lord. Continuing to pray this
way has helped me maintain my submission to
Jesus as Lord.

Another important prayer is "Lord, I serve at
your pleasure. Use me, or not, whatever pleases
you." This prayer emerged from observing military
leaders. They impress me with their obedience to
orders. They understand they do not deserve any
special assignment and are willing to serve without
recognition. They serve to accomplish the mission
as ordered by their commander.

Meditating on this kind of obedience one
morning, it dawned on me how arrogant some of
my praying was. I usually prayed "Lord, use me
today" as if he were somehow obligated to do so.
After all, I am his willing servant, so therefore he
has to use me. God showed me how arrogant that
prayer really was. My prayer of genuine submission became "Lord, use me . . . or not, whatever
pleases you."

That is the issue, isn't it? Whatever pleases God
and advances his mission is what is important—not
that we be used! Sometimes, God does not use a
person for awhile as part of his purpose for them.
Even Paul, the most effective Christian missionary
and writer of all time, experienced this. Paul was
busy in mission service when he was arrested and
entangled in the Roman legal system. While at the

peak of his ministry effectiveness and influence, Acts 24:27 records, "After two years had passed . . . Felix left Paul in prison."

Are you kidding me?! How can that be? The most effective missionary/theologian in history was left in prison for two years while a low-ranking Roman ruler waited for a bribe to release him. How could that have happened? Why not another earthquake, like the one in Philippi (Acts 16:16–40) which set Paul free earlier in his ministry? The answer, the only answer that makes sense, is God wanted Paul to wait in prison. This was his purpose for Paul. His assignment was to wait until God was ready for him to go to Rome. Sometimes, God accomplishes his purpose by not using us the way we imagine he should, the way that seems logical, or the way that makes the most sense to us.

A third prayer that reminds me of Jesus' Lordship is "Lord, your kingdom matters. Mine doesn't. Advance your cause, whatever that means for me." This prayer emerged from the pressure I felt to provide for my family, send my children to college, save for retirement, invest in my home, and build my estate.

One day it occurred to me how much time I was spending on my kingdom. Then God got really personal. He unveiled how much of my ministry was really self-centered as well. So much of my effort was about the wrong kingdom!

Striking balance in this area is tough. We have God-assigned responsibilities for our families, ministry, and work. But our focus must be on building the kingdom of God, not building our own kingdom. Jesus warned of this in Luke 12. The rich young fool prospered and all he could think of was "building bigger barns." God wants us to be careful that our focus is not building bigger barns but is instead using what's in those barns for his purposes.

Finally, the fourth prayer that creates a spiritual foundation for integrity is "Lord, you are God. I am not. Help me keep that straight today." I enjoy umpiring baseball. I like to joke that the reason I enjoy umpiring is "All week long I serve God; on Saturday I get to play God." That's funny about umpiring. It's not funny about life.

I am not God. You are not either. We often act like we are. We worry about things above our pay grade. We take responsibility for outcomes we cannot control. We expect to change people. In short, we play God.

This prayer helps me remember that God is God, Jesus is God, the Holy Spirit is God. I am not God. I never will be and I need to stop acting like it.

These prayers are centering prayers for me. They bring me back to the central reality "Jesus is my Lord." Remembering that fundamental spiritual reality is essential to maintaining integrity. Use these prayers, or, better, write some short prayers from your own experiences that remind you that Jesus is Lord. Pray them often to help keep you centered on this fundamental spiritual reality!

2. I am a steward accountable to Jesus as Lord (Luke 16:1–15; 1 Cor. 4:1–2)

Usually, stewardship is equated with managing money. That's unfortunate because the concept is much larger than money. The principle or concept of stewardship impacts many areas of life. For example, Jesus was clear in Matthew 28:18 when he said that "all authority" had been given to him. All means all. Jesus has all authority in the universe. Whatever authority we have, he has shared with us. It's still his and that makes us stewards or managers of it, not owners.

The Bible teaches that Jesus delegates his authority through structures and people. For example, parents have authority in families; rulers have authority in governments; leaders have authority in churches. Paul wrote about ministry leaders, "A person should consider us in this way: as servants of Christ and managers [stewards] of God's mysteries" (1 Cor. 4:1). A steward is someone who manages what belongs to another person.

In the context of leadership, this is clear. Jesus has all authority. He shares it with leaders to whom he assigns roles in his kingdom. So then, as a leader, Jesus has made you a steward of some of his leadership authority and responsibility. You are a leader but only because Jesus has put you in charge of a little part of his kingdom. He expects you to handle with care the responsibility he has given you. It is his church or ministry you are leading.

There are three stark realities about your current position that will help you keep your leadership stewardship in perspective. These may surprise or disappoint you at first! But they are true, and truth is never discouraging. Reality is not depressing, although it may make you adjust your thinking.

The three realities about your current position are:

1. You are only the current occupant of your leadership role.
2. You are always a temporary employee.
3. You are a transition person for your job.

I warned you! These sound like belittling statements, but they are not. They are simply the truth and provide some needed perspective to the cultural tendency to puff up leaders with titles, salaries, and perks that communicate importance.

As I write this, I am a seminary president. While I hope to serve for many years, I am not the last president the seminary will ever have (unless Jesus comes soon!). My role is a stewardship of leadership

Jesus has given me. A good man had it before me. A good man will have it after me. I am only a caretaker of the position and the authority that comes with it. The job really belongs to Jesus! He is only sharing this leadership role with me for a short time.

You are in the same situation. You are only the current pastor, minister, director, board member, or staff member of whatever you are assigned to lead. The job is not yours. It belongs to the Lord. He is only sharing it with you for awhile and he expects you to take care of it.

You are a temporary worker. Most organizations use "temps" from time to time. But in reality, all of us are temps. We are assigned for a season, not forever. We are also transitional. Many churches use "interim pastors" during their time between permanent pastors. But in reality, we are all interims! There is usually someone before us and after us.

If you have difficulty believing any of this, imagine what would happen if you died suddenly. There would be grieving, mourning, and probably a nice memorial service. Someone might put up a memorial plaque or name something for you. Then they would replace you and life would go on! It really would. You are not as indispensable as you think you are.

As stewards, we have a responsibility that transcends our unique time of leadership. We are responsible to use what is not ours, our leadership

role, and make the most effective contribution possible. That's not demeaning; that's reality. Keeping
this in focus will help you maintain integrity. You
will remember the job is not yours, the salary is
not deserved, the perks will not last, and it's not all
about you. You are a steward, so take care of the
Lord's work and lead it carefully.

3. I am in an authority structure affirmed by Jesus as Lord (Rom. 13:1–7; Matt. 28:18)

Part of maintaining integrity is understanding
authority structures—knowing to whom you are
accountable, who is accountable to you, and how
these relationships create needed boundaries in
your life. Jesus has all authority and he shares his
authority through appropriate structures. He has
all kinds of people in authority, in my case trust-
ees, who supervise part of his work. I have a Boss
(Jesus) who has given me some bosses (the trust-
ees). While you may have a different structure, you
have one nonetheless!

Jesus works through authority structures.
He expects his leaders to work under and within
authority structures he puts in their lives. This is
not always pleasant or easy, but it is a part of maintaining integrity by creating boundaries. Many
churches and ministry organizations are fuzzy at
this point. Clear lines of authority are not delin-
eated. Leaders who encounter cloudy organiza-

tional structures must insist that authority structures are clarified, not for the purpose of control but to free leaders from unrealistic expectations and unreasonable demands. As a leader, you deserve to know to whom you are responsible and what you are responsible for.

When we learn to trust Jesus to work through others to correct, guide, and direct us, we will grow in integrity. We need others to help us manage our lives and to stay in line. Admitting that is a big step for some leaders. You may feel that those with authority in your church or organization are incompetent, do not know as much as you do about leadership, or do not know how to adequately supervise you. All that may be true, but you are still responsible to work within the authority structure Jesus has allowed in your life. You can resign or renegotiate accountability relationships, but you cannot rebel against them and be successful over the long haul.

So, what does this look like, practically, in a ministry organization? How can you structure relationships with your supervisors and supervisees to promote integrity? Here are some suggestions.

Professional relationships can make a positive difference in maintaining integrity. Often, leaders must foster these relationships because of reluctance by followers or peers to question the leaders' actions or motives. Simple steps can be taken to make yourself accountable to people at work.

First, insist that your supervisors have a specific plan to evaluate you annually and that it be done. Routine supervision, when problems can be addressed in a matter-of-fact process, is much better than crisis supervision only invoked when problems arise. Many pastors have no such structure. Many Christian organizations feel this is "too corporate." Nothing could be less corporate and more Christian than defining boundaries and expectations and then treating people fairly!

Pastors must insist that an accountability structure be clearly identified in their church. This sometimes means the pastor is in the awkward position of forming this group, training it, and then submitting to its direction. Though it may be awkward, it must be done. Every pastor deserves this kind of support/supervision group. When it is functioning well, it gives a pastor a powerful sense of confidence, blessing, and accomplishment.

Having good supervision helps maintain integrity in several ways. First, it corrects problems when they are small. Second, it promotes dialogue and mutual support for leaders. Third, it helps leaders learn about themselves and analyze their motives. And finally, leaders have good feedback about how they are perceived by others.

A second step to improve integrity through professional relationships is to make yourself accountable for your whereabouts. I grew up around men who bragged, "I come and go as I please." That attitude led to bad choices for many of them and leads to disastrous choices for leaders. I implement this principle by informing my assistant of my schedule and updating changes as they happen. She always knows where I am, who I am with, and how to reach me. This keeps anyone from wondering about my workload, questioning my work habits, wondering if I am someplace I am not supposed to be, or with someone I am not supposed to be with. By volunteering this information, I let everyone know I do not mind being held accountable. No secrets!

Third, make yourself accountable for your use of money. Our chief financial officer and controller review my expense report monthly. They must both agree to its fitness before it is accepted. If either of them questions any item, it gets pulled off the report with no appeal from me. Our board, finance committee, and audit committee monitor other financial decisions.

When I was a pastor, a lay person always made this same kind of evaluation before reimbursements were allowed. Throughout my ministry, I have insisted that someone else evaluate my personal use of reimbursable funds. Needless to say, it is also important to create and submit to proper procedures for use of all ministry funds.

I have heard ministry leaders say, "If you trust me to teach you the Word of God, you should trust me to handle the money without looking over my shoulder." Red flag! That arrogant attitude will destroy integrity. Find out how to account for every dollar in your ministry . . . and do it! Safeguards must be put in place, documentation must be produced, and care must be taken to be completely above reproach when it comes to money. Obtaining purchase orders, keeping receipts, filling out forms, and operating within a budget can seem onerous. But do it! Do all of it! Keep yourself straight with money.

Fourth, account for your decisions. Leaders make decisions. It's what we do. Leaders are not paid by the hour or the job. We are paid to make good decisions. When you make a decision, own up to it. You will make some bad decisions. Do not compound a bad decision by another one—shifting the blame or denying the responsibility for your decision. Real leaders avoid scapegoating or passing the buck.

Once, in a different ministry, I made a decision in direct violation of a board directive. My next move was to call the board chairman and tell him what I had done and why. The next time the board met, I told the full board of my actions and why. Their response was to affirm my decision, confirm the validity of my reasons, and to caution me not to take their approval for carte blanche permission in the future.

There are times when rules must be broken. When that time comes, the reasons will be acceptable to most reasonable people. While you will not need to justify your actions, you are required to explain them and own them. In a later chapter on courage, you will learn how to stand alone with a decision—even against your supporters—and absorb the consequences. But most of the time, our actions and their results are not that dramatic. The drama usually occurs when we crawfish away from our responsibility or shift the blame for our decisions to others. Do not do it. Integrity demands a better response.

Integrity is promoted by living in authority structures. Do not complicate this simple principle. Allow the people God has placed around you, organizationally, to promote integrated living. Learn to cooperate with the accountability systems, structures, and procedures. If you sense rebellion building within you, be careful! It is very easy to justify marginal choices that then lead to sinful choices and compromised integrity.

Spiritual Disciplines for Developing Integrity

A second significant part of developing and maintaining integrity is practicing spiritual disciplines throughout your lifetime. Spiritual disciplines build structure into our lives. They anchor us to core activities that, over time, produce transforming results.

Practicing spiritual disciplines is like building a brick house. You lay the first brick and you do not have much of a house. But over time, you can build a solid structure with incremental, disciplined effort—laying one brick at a time. Spiritual disciplines build our lives one day at a time. They are also like a small stream wearing away a giant rock. Spiritual disciplines wear away our impurities and imperfections. There are at least four core spiritual disciplines essential to maintaining integrity, although other disciplines are also helpful.

Devotional Bible Reading

You must read the Bible regularly, asking God for wisdom, insight, and direction. This differs from studying the Bible for preaching, teaching, or other ministry. It is easier to study the Bible for what it says to someone else! You must discipline yourself to read and study the Bible *personally.* You must ask, "God, what do you want to say to *me?*"

For years, I have been systematically reading the Bible. I read it when I feel good and when I do not, when God seems close and when he seems far away, when I want to and when I do not, when I am "getting something out of it" and when I am not. Through all this, I just keep reading the Bible.

I know that this discipline is foundational to God's keeping me on track with him.

My mother owns a beautiful cutting horse. This horse makes working cattle look like magic. Just a slight brush of the reins is all that is required for instant response to my mother's directions. Contrast that with an old mule that has to be dragged into action. Daily Bible reading gives God opportunity for incremental, gentle correction. We must keep short accounts! We ask God to speak each day and we respond accordingly rather than depending on a sporadic, cataclysmic response to keep us on track.

Be a cutting horse, not a mule.

Devotional Prayer

You must pray regularly for yourself, for personal needs, and for personal spiritual focus. As a leader, you will pray often for others. You must also discipline yourself to pray about your own life. This kind of prayer is more difficult. Meditation and introspection is always more difficult than intercession. Asking God to work in us and on us is always harder than asking him to work through us for someone else.

Part of this process is asking God to reveal sin in your life and then confessing and repenting of it. Part of it is meditating on insights from Scripture in your Bible reading and praying about applying those insights. This can also include personal needs, fears, concerns, and requests. But, most of all, it is personal. Again, keep short accounts! Get right with God often.

Sabbath Rest

Resting one day out of every seven is an essential spiritual discipline to maintain integrity for several reasons. First, it humbles you by showing your followers you are human and you recognize your own limitations. Second, it affirms your faith that God can do more in six days than you can do working seven. Third, it refreshes you physically so you are less prone to mistakes tired people make. Fourth, it models submission to God by following his model of working six days and resting one. Finally, it restores your perspective and prepares you for further ministry.

I know several ministry leaders who have had some major failure of integrity—often a moral failure. In almost every case, burnout was part of the problem. In a fatigued state, leaders make choices they would not otherwise make. One pastor justified stealing church funds by saying, "I had not taken any time off in two years. They worked me so hard I felt they owed me the money." This was a well-respected, effective leader. He made a bad choice, not because "they worked me so hard" but because *he* had worked too much. Burnout often leads to disintegrating integrity.

Sabbath rest is difficult to establish and maintain for many leaders. To help you make a practical plan, chapter ten has a more detailed discussion of implementing this important practice.

Worship Attendance

Public worship is a primary way God confronts us. We need worship leaders to speak truth to us, to lead us to express ourselves through music and prayer in ways we would not otherwise choose, and to call us to fresh obedience through giving, repenting, and making commitments.

This may seem like the easiest discipline to practice! Many Christian leaders lead multiple worship services weekly. But that is the problem. As we lead, we are rightly more concerned with the worshippers than we are with our own response to God. Every leader occasionally needs to be a worshipper, not a worship leader.

Conferences abound for Christian leaders. You may attend them, but do you go with a focused purpose to hear from God? That is the challenge. Discipline yourself to become a worshipper, choosing opportunities to open yourself to God in public services. If you lead worship or preach in a church with multiple services, perhaps you can occasionally attend a service as a worshipper. These experiences allow God to probe and prod, to call you to fresh sacrifice and commitment. And, with

integrity, to respond publicly to invitations as God
directs. What's good for the people you lead to
worship is good for you too!

———◆———

Integrity is the lifelong challenge of bringing your behavior in line with biblical standards.
Maintaining integrity is a continuing process, a
never-ending quest to live your values in every
area of life. As you live an integrated life, you will
engender trust from your followers and build a
leadership legacy that will not diminish over time
or be washed away by character failure.

You have remarkable resources for building
an integrated life. Spiritual resources like those
described above create a firm foundation. Spiritual
disciplines, those listed here and others such as
fasting and Scripture memory, provide incremental
correction and direction. The quest to build an integrated life, to be called a man or woman of integrity,
is the worthy goal that can be accomplished.

Maintaining integrity is a lifelong process.
Pursue it with passion!

CHAPTER THREE

Finding Security

AFTER INTEGRITY, THE most important character quality for any leader who wants to make
a significant impact and leave a positive legacy is
security. Yet, security is seldom listed in job pro-
files as a desired quality. Secure leaders know who
they are and what God has made them to do. They
understand their strengths and weaknesses and are
comfortable with both. Secure leaders feel less pressure to perform, less pressure to please people, and
less pressure to prove their worth by their accomplishments than insecure leaders do. Secure leaders
have an ease about them that engenders confidence
among their followers. And, secure leaders attract
strong leaders to work with them because they are
not afraid to share the work and the rewards.

Many leaders are high achievers or overachiev-
ers. Often overachievement is a mask for deep insecurity. Insecurity, for many of us, is rooted in the

psychological and emotional scars incurred during childhood. Many Christian leaders, including many high performance leaders, come from broken or dysfunctional families. Much could be written about the causes of insecurity, including these and others. But for our purposes, analyzing the causes is not essential. Let's agree with the obvious! Insecurity affects most of us. Leaders, no matter how gifted, are not exempt.

The Search for Security

The search for security is a primal human urge. That truth is self-evident. People, including leaders, want to and need to feel secure. We often go to great lengths in our search for security. The problem is we frequently pursue wrong sources for security. We look for security in accomplishment and relationships, often with catastrophic results.

A good example of this was the woman Jesus met at the well (John 4). She asked Jesus a question about religious achievement: "Where should we worship?" Jesus replied with a question about the whereabouts of her husband. This prompted her admission of multiple marriages and adultery. Her pattern of searching for security in relationships was unveiled.

Jesus did not answer her question about religious accomplishment (proper worship) or con-

front her misplaced search for security in relationships (serial marriages). Instead, he addressed her
deepest needs. He promised he would come into her
life and quench her deepest thirsts. He portrayed
himself as a spring of "living water." He challenged
her to stop drawing from wrong wells and to come
to the true source of inner satisfaction.

Most people, including many leaders, look
for security in accomplishments or relationships.
Christian leaders make this more palatable by
searching for security in religious accomplishments
or religious relationships. Neither ultimately satisfies. A better source for security is available to every
Christian leader.

First, however, it is important to diagnose the
problem by revealing the symptoms of insecurity as they express themselves in leaders. Starting
with a negative analysis may be discouraging. But
before you can solve the problem, you must diagnose it. Many leaders have unhealthy behavior they
would like to stop. They have patterns or habits
that undermine their success. Yet, some inner drive
repeatedly motivates the same destructive actions.
That powerful inner drive is your search for security expressing itself in unhealthy ways.

So, here are some of the symptoms of an insecure leader. If you have any of these symptoms,
you will feel some dis-ease as you read! But that
unsettledness can motivate significant change as

you become more secure. Leading out of security, rather than insecurity, is essential to leaving a positive leadership legacy.

How Insecurity Expresses Itself in Leaders

Insecurity is a root cause of many symptoms that express themselves in dysfunctional behavior by leaders. Many times leaders work hard on symptom management—trying to solve these problems—without addressing the underlying cause. They go to conferences, read books, go for counseling, or earn another degree to no avail. This breeds frustration and greater dysfunction as leaders fail to permanently change their behavior. You may be feeling this frustration. The solution is to analyze your symptoms and discover their true source. Stop treating symptoms and cure the cause.

So, how does insecurity express itself in leaders? How can you recognize the telltale signs of an insecure leader? What outward evidence gives away the inner insecurity that drives someone who appears so successful?

Symptom 1: The inability to say no without feeling guilty. Leaders have many demands placed on them. Saying no to requests for appointments, for requests to attend meetings or community activities, to fund-raising appeals, and to demanding church members is difficult. Some leaders struggle with saying no because of the deep sense of fulfillment and value they receive from saying yes.

One pastor told me that every time church members called, no matter what they wanted, he felt obligated to respond. He told me of repeated instances when he would be sitting down with a bowl of popcorn to watch a movie with his family or preparing to go to his son's ball game or dressing for an evening out with his wife and the phone would ring. Off he would go, usually in a nonemergency situation, to meet the immediate "need" of the caller. This pastor simply could not say no. He was addicted to the affirmation people gave him for being such a high-performance pastor.

This was a competent, intelligent, effective pastor who was leading a growing church. He told me, "I think we can grow to 1,000. That's about how many people I can take care of." By "take care of," he meant "personally attend to." I challenged him to consider his ministry style, what was driving him, the long-term impact on his family and his health. He assured me: "It's all under control. And after all, God has called me to sacrifice for my people."

This pastor had grown up in an abusive home with little or no affirmation from his father. He was rewarded for his spiritual zeal as a teenager by well-meaning church members and soon became addicted to Christian service. Combined with natural charisma, intelligence, and excellent speaking skills, he seemed like the ideal pastor—the kind of hard-working, hard-praying, hard-preaching man of God every church wants.

Over time, his wife became disillusioned and discouraged with his neglect and warped understanding of ministry. She insisted he devote more time to her and their children. He promised to do better, but like an alcoholic drawn to the bottle, he could not break his ministry habit. He needed his "affirmation fix" daily to meet his deep insecurity. He craved the sense of belonging, importance, and value that came from admiring church members. After awhile his wife stopped asking for his attention and started acting defiantly. Her behavior became erratic and out of character. Outsiders questioned her "rebellion." Insiders knew she was not the problem.

All this came to a head when his wife, desperate for the attention her husband could not and would not give her, left him for another man. Some blamed her for being an adulteress (and, yes, she was). But few knew the whole story. This family came apart not because of a woman's lust but because of the unsatisfied thirst of an insecure pastor.

One symptom of insecurity in your life may be the inability to say no without feeling guilty. You crave the admiration, affirmation, or even adulation others give you. You have a deep thirst for security, as all of us do, but you are satisfying it in destructive ways. You are unable to say no. Secure leaders, on the other hand, can say no because they are not dependent on constant affirmation from others.

Symptom 2: The inability to take risks and fail. Leaders are decision makers who are willing to take risks and possibly fail. Having the "high failure tolerance gene" is necessary for any leader who innovates, changes paradigms, or attempts new ventures.

Yet, some leaders become immobilized at this point. They are unable to take risks because of fear of failure, of what people will think, or of losing status in their church or community. They often wonder, *How will this decision make me look if it fails?* These leaders are status conscious, not because of pride but because their fragile sense of security cannot tolerate much failure.

One young minister withered in his ability to take risks. He made some decisions early in a new ministry that were not popular. They were good decisions that produced solid results, but they were unpopular decisions. The critics nibbled at him like a thousand gnats. Over time, this young leader became more and more wary. He was unwilling to make decisions because he could not stand the "ego hit" of the criticism that would come his way. Eventually, he simply froze! He stopped leading entirely.

You may be like this. You may have been more willing to take risks and make decisions earlier in your ministry. But the critics wore you down! Now you gauge the wind before every decision. You wonder how people will respond (normal course of consideration for a leader) but base your decision on how you will feel after they respond (a symptom that you have a security problem).

Everyone wants to be liked. That's not the issue. The problem is avoiding decisions, risk, and possible failure in order to avoid displeasing people. You crave the security that favor with others provides and you are unwilling to do anything to jeopardize those relationships. A former college president told me he had difficulty recruiting businessmen to serve on his board with pastors. Why? The lay leaders were frustrated with pastors' inability to make unpopular decisions because they are notorious people-pleasers. While that may sting, it is unfortunately true too much of the time.

Insecure leaders are immobilized by possible failure. Secure leaders make decisions, including those fraught with potential failure, concerned for but not controlled by the opinions of others.

Symptom 3: The inability to trust others to make decisions. Sponsoring conferences to train ministry leaders to recruit, delegate, and involve people was part of my ministry for years. I watched well-intentioned leaders fill notebooks with helpful suggestions to make them better managers. Yet, few seemed to ever implement any of this material in life-changing patterns for ministry. What gives?

The problem for many leaders is not lack of knowledge. They know good leaders recruit volunteers or employ staff to enlarge their organization. They know how to motivate and train people to do ministry, how to create neat organizational charts on their computers, and how to structure a well-oiled ministry machine.

But something keeps them from doing these things. That something is insecurity. Many leaders simply cannot empower others to do ministry and make meaningful decisions about their ministry. Sometimes, the problem is the followers are not trustworthy. Sometimes, the followers really are not competent. In either of those cases, the wise leader will reserve decision-making responsibility. But, more often, the real problem is the leader does not want to give up this positional perk.

Making decisions means you get the credit for good decisions and can avoid the blame for bad decisions you prevent. Both of these relate to the previous two symptoms of insecurity. You want the credit for every decision because you need the affirmation to feel secure in yourself. You avoid the pain of bad decisions because you are not secure enough to handle the resulting criticism.

As a young pastor, I attended every deacons' meeting and every committee meeting of our church. Nothing happened without my brilliant input! After all, I *was* the pastor. I was twenty-four years old, knew very little about many of the issues being decided, but was desperately in need of appearing to be in charge. My insecurities drove me to be everywhere! I wanted the credit for the good things I was sure would happen and I wanted to prevent anything bad from happening.

Two experiences started changing my thinking. The first was Vacation Bible School. As a former minister to children, I had an idea what our small church could probably achieve with this program. Just after I arrived at the church, a woman came to my office and said, "It's my year to be VBS director. Another woman and I alternate years. If it's all right with you we'll get started soon. I think we can have about 200 children this year."

I almost laughed out loud. Any more than 100 would be a miracle. But I thought, *I'll let her do it her way. By next year, I'm sure they will want me to step in and do it right.* Over 200 children came! What a shock to me! Other people could do very effective ministry without my coaching. She actually knew more about VBS than I did.

In that same church, we went through a prolonged long-range planning process. My hands were all over it. Not one detail made it through the process without my scrutiny and approval. When it was presented, it almost split the church. The business meeting to consider it was one of the worst experiences of my ministry. It was a superb example of what happened with more of my "brilliant" input.

From these experiences, and numerous others, God began showing me my presence was not required at every church meeting. And, what was more painful, he began showing me the real reason I thought my presence was required. My insecurities were driving me, overcoming both my training and my intuitive sense of how to lead effectively.

These early experiences benefited my church planting experience that followed my first pastorate. We moved to a suburb of Portland, Oregon, and planted a new church. By this time I was beginning to confront my insecurities and change my behavior. From the very beginning, I shared the leadership of the church with others, including people I had only known for a few weeks. Some of those early leaders had not been Christians very long when they were given real responsibility and empowered to make decisions. While they occasionally made bad decisions, most of the time they made very good ones.

The ability to share leadership, to delegate and empower, was growing in proportion to the security I was developing in Jesus Christ. Several times I left leaders' meetings or other church meetings to coach my children in various sports, each time saying, "Whatever you decide, I'm with you." We also implemented a task force structure that enabled me to train groups at the beginning of an assignment and meet with them only at their request or when they finished a project. For several years we developed our budget, mission strategies, youth and children's programs, and other projects using this model. Dozens, if not hundreds, of meetings and decisions happened without my direct involvement, and the church was better for it.

This change was possible because of my growing security as a person and as a leader. An insecure leader struggles to empower others for shared leadership and decision making. Conversely, secure leaders trust others to lead and make decisions.

Symptom 4: The inability to keep work in perspective. Men, in particular, often define themselves by what they do. When men first meet one another, one of the get-acquainted questions is often, "What do you do?" Very often we allow what we do to define who we are. Our security issues, and often our esteem needs, are satisfied through production at work.

This can be a major problem for men in Christian leadership. We do not produce an easily defined product. At the end of the day, we often have few tangible results to show. Our business is transformed lives, and that is a very slow, nebulous process. We do not have a clear bottom line.

Some leaders cannot handle this frustrating reality. Their insecurity forces them to find a way to keep score, to notch their belt to give them a sense of accomplishment. One way of doing this is working long hours to gain approval or prove your worth. Another way is working to stay busy, rather than being productive. Finally, some make sure their work, and its results, is well publicized. Counseling sessions, late night hospital trips, and how you solve thorny church problems just happen to be mentioned in Sunday sermons or pastoral newsletter columns. Baptism, budget, and building achievements are prominently reported—but only during good years!

Leaders struggle to keep work in perspective because of their insecurities. Ministry leaders who compare themselves to the work accomplishments of men in their community are prone to this. Those men are producing products, increasing their bottom line, growing their revenue, improving their earnings, and otherwise achieving measurable success. Christian leaders want the same respect, appreciation, and ego-salving satisfaction others seem to receive.

This symptom manifests itself in the subtle temptation to find security in material possessions. Many Christian leaders, particularly in the United States, are able to work vocationally in ministry and be compensated adequately. Some are even compensated generously. One pastor said, "I don't know where the top is in ministry, but I'm headed toward it as fast as I can go." He believed that hard work would produce promotions and financial reward. He's right. They often do in a capitalistic system.

But Christian leaders cannot be motivated by financial success. It leads to false security and disillusionment with ministry. We must model a better understanding of work, productivity, personal gain, and security. Ambition for the right purposes and under the Lord's authority is admirable. Unbridled lust for monetary gain to give you a sense of security and personal worth is not.

Another related problem that reveals insecurity is the inability to celebrate the success of other ministry leaders. Criticizing others who are experiencing God's blessings reveals our character flaws, not those of the people we are demeaning. Secure leaders have solved these problems: They have a healthy, balanced perspective on their work. They can celebrate the success of others. While work accomplishments are important, they are not their source of security.

Analysis and diagnosis is not enough. Perhaps you have connected these symptoms to insecurity as the root cause for the first time. So now, what do you do about these symptoms?

Find Security in Jesus Christ

When my insecurities became so obvious they could no longer be ignored, the questions became, "What do I do about them? How do I find genuine security?" And, the more basic question, "Is it wrong to want to feel secure?"

The desires for security and significance are not sub-Christian. God has made every person with the same basic desires and drives. There is nothing wrong with wanting to feel secure. The problem is we often satisfy this deep longing in destructive ways. Perhaps you have seen yourself in the earlier description of symptoms of insecurity in a leader. The solution is not eradicating your need to feel secure. The solution is finding security from a proper source.

A basic doctrine of the Christian faith is the security of the believer. I grew up in a part of the country populated by influential churches that did not believe this doctrine. I heard many passionate debates about "once saved, always saved" between Baptists and friends from other groups. That was my early exposure to the security of the believer. The focus was on eternity. If you were saved now, you would be saved forever. My early understanding of this doctrine meant it was more about tomorrow than it is about today.

Understanding my need for personal security drove me to reconsider the doctrine of the security of the believer. After significant study, this break-through came in my understanding: *The security of the believer is as much about today as it is about eternity.* The security of the believer means that all who trust Jesus for salvation will always be secure with him. But it also means we are as secure *now* as we will ever be. Your security in Jesus is not something you get when you die. You received it when you were saved. You are as secure in Jesus right now as you will ever be.

The security of the believer is not a cold, sterile doctrine to be debated. It is a present spiritual reality to be enjoyed! The beginning point of overcoming insecurity is renewing your mind with biblical truth about your security in Jesus. Your security as a believer, particularly as it relates to leadership, can be summarized in the following key statements.

God and Jesus make you secure. In John 10:28–29, believers are portrayed as being held tightly in Jesus' hands. Jesus and all believers are portrayed as being held tightly in God's hands. Jesus promises "no one is able to snatch them out of the Father's hand" and that he and the Father "are one." This imagery means God guarantees your secure relationship with him through Jesus Christ. This simple conviction is the foundation of your security as a believer: God and Jesus hold you securely in relationship with them.

That is comforting! Your security comes from your relationship with God. You are not responsible for your security, for somehow finding emotional health that produces security, or creating a sense of personal security. You are secure because God has secured you to himself. He has given you identity and infused you with value as his child.

Security emerges from a relationship. We seem to know that intuitively. Seeking security in wrong relationships is the problem. Doing this ultimately causes leaders to abuse relationships. We might compulsively serve people to gain their approval and blessing. We might develop an immoral relationship seeking inner satisfaction. Or, we might compromise inappropriately to keep our job.

Right principle, wrong applications! You *should* seek security in a relationship but in the right relationship—with God through Jesus. Seeking it in any other relationship—your wife, child, mother, father, or followers—will leave you empty and longing. Like a sugar high, it may satisfy for awhile but will leave you deflated.

The only source of real security is your relationship with God through Jesus. He validates you, blesses you, accepts you, and gives you worth. In him, you *are* secure so you can choose to live securely and feel secure.

True security resists all threats. Jesus made two other promises in John 10:28–29 related to our security. He promised that we are so secure "no one" can harm us and we have "eternal life." This has two applications related to your security.

First, no one can take away the security you have in God through Jesus. You will be tested repeatedly and often at this point. Leaders sometimes deal with difficult people. We are criticized, ridiculed, and rejected. Our proposals are analyzed, dissected, and vilified. People offer "constructive criticism" on what we wear, drive, and do in our leisure time. They comment on how we raise our children, comb our hair, and maintain our homes. No area is exempt from the prying eyes and sharp comment of someone.

One pastor announced to his church that he and his wife were adopting their first child. Afterward, one matron congratulated him and said, "That is the best way for every pastor to get his children" (as opposed to the "other" way). Nothing in a leader's life seems off limits from public comment.

More serious critics write poisonous letters, make appointments to formally rebuke you, gossip aggressively, or otherwise attack you publicly. No matter how strong you are or how unfounded the attacks, they still hurt. Critics rob insecure leaders of their sense of God's abiding blessing. While feeling the emotional sting of criticism, secure leaders are not controlled by their critics. They rest in the security they have in the one relationship that really matters.

Second, this security is forever. Remember, it is not for the afterlife only, but for this life as well. Specifically, no matter what the present or future holds, you are and always will be secure. You can live through public criticism, loss of status, bad decisions, and other personal attacks because you are secure. You can also survive personal loss, family illness, financial setbacks or whatever else the future has in store for you. Your security in your relationship with God through Jesus can stand up to anything that comes at you.

This is the great, often untapped reality of the security of the believer. You are as secure in Jesus *right now* as you will ever be. You are as secure now as you will someday be in heaven. You *are* secure . . . so live it and enjoy it!

Secure leaders are free to obey God. When Jesus taught about our security, he also said his followers listen to his voice and follow him (John 10:27). Jesus recognized an important reality: People are often controlled by their need for security. Security is such a strong need, compelling drive, and powerful thirst, that whatever satisfies the need will be obeyed. Leaders who draw security from God through Jesus are free to obey God.

One young leader's deep insecurity led him into Internet pornography. Looking at graphic sexual images gave him a satisfaction he did not experience in other ways, not even in a sexual relationship with his wife. He mistakenly thought the intense, but brief emotional release he felt while viewing pornography would satisfy his deep inner longings. In short, in a twisted yet powerful way, he looked to pornography to prove his manhood and establish his security.

No matter how sinful he felt, how much self-condemnation he experienced, or how many times he promised God he would never do it again, his compulsive pattern only deepened. Ultimately, an emotional breakdown resulted. The steady love of his wife, the wise counsel of elders, a no-nonsense accountability group, and the support of his church created the environment for him to change his behavior. But, the behavior only changed when he realized Internet pornography was not his problem. Pornography was his symptom. Deep insecurity was his problem.

You *will* satisfy your thirst for security. The drive for security is not the problem. How we satisfy it is. If people liking you makes you feel secure, you will please people at all costs. If accomplishments make you feel secure, you will be driven to get things done. If physical pleasure, however fleeting, gives you a sense of security, you will pursue those passions. You will obey the compelling urge that feeds your need for security. But, if your relationship with God through Jesus is your source of security, you will obey God.

Secure leaders are confident without being arrogant. They are relaxed without being lackadaisical. Secure leaders rest in the reality that their relationship with God is their defining source of value, worth, and well-being. They have nothing left to prove, nothing left to conquer, and are not beholden to anyone. Secure leaders are free to obey God—and there is no greater freedom!

Renewing Your Mind, Really Feeling Secure

Changing a core understanding like your source of security happens at both a point in time and as a process over time. It starts by accepting the truth that the only legitimate source of security is a relationship with God through Jesus Christ. That is a "point in time" decision you must make based on truth—revealed, absolute, nonnegotiable truth from the Bible.

Hammering down that stake, affirming your conviction about your security is the first step. The second step is more challenging. You must practice the spiritual discipline of confronting wrong thinking, destructive behavior, and bad habits built on your foundation of false security. This requires meditation, prayer, reflection, accountability, and difficult choices. Foundational to these disciplines is renewing your mind through Scripture memory. Choose key passages about your security in Jesus Christ and commit them to memory. Allow them to reprogram your thinking—to renew your mind—and give you a new outlook on yourself and what gives you true worth. When you do this, real change will come through real choices.

For me, this meant making an intentional choice to give up some decision-making responsibilities and attending every church meeting. It was a choice to trust people and live with mistakes that would be made. It was making a specific choice to be less controlling, realizing my personal worth was not determined by the actions or opinions of others. For me, this meant relaxing as a parent and making decisions about my children based on their welfare, not what others thought of me as a parent. It means critics are an ever-present reality but their criticism does not define who I am, how I must respond, what I must do, or how I feel about myself as a leader.

These are specific examples of me facing the hard reality that insecurity motivated my actions. Insecurity was driving me both to control people and please them inappropriately. It was a toxic mix!

These are frank admissions. Now, what about you? Will you be as honest with yourself and with

God? What are you doing that reveals a wrong source of security? Will you change? How will you change?

Do not be discouraged if this is a prolonged process. I still pray often, meditating on Scripture affirming my security in Jesus, and asking for strength to make decisions in obedience to him alone. Temptation entices me to give in to old patterns. But the good news is those temptations are waning as years of walking in new truth about security creates new and better habits.

God wants you to be secure in him and lead out of that powerful certainty. Break the bondage of insecurity and devilish false security from sources that can never satisfy. Become a secure leader in Jesus Christ.

CHAPTER FOUR

Maintaining Purity

NO FAILURE IS more devastating to ministry leaders, their followers, and their families than moral failure. Ministry leaders represent God, and are therefore expected to be honorable in personal relationships. Ministers are (or at least used to be) trusted to be morally pure and represent a standard of moral purity. We have positions of power and influence in our communities and certainly within our churches or ministries. We often work with people when they are most vulnerable. When leaders in positions of spiritual power exploit those vulnerabilities, the results are catastrophic.

Surely, there is more to personal purity than sexual or moral fidelity. But this problem is so significant among ministry leaders that it deserves a special focus. Building moral purity and protecting it over a lifetime is essential for your present effectiveness and positive leadership legacy.

Confronted!

"I can't believe another Christian television minister has confessed to immorality," I lamented. My friend, a man about my age, and I were commiserating about another fallen minister. "That guy is such a jerk. What he did, I would never do. It could never happen to me."

Those words snapped my friend to attention. He leaned across my desk and said, quietly but very clearly, "Jeff, those are the most dangerous words I have ever heard you say. If you think it can't happen to you, you are more vulnerable than you can imagine. It can happen, and it will happen, unless you keep up a careful guard."

His intensity startled me and made my blood run cold! He had nailed me. My arrogance was showing. This crack in my character could become a fatal flaw that would destroy me. That night I realized I was more vulnerable to moral failure than I had been willing to admit. I determined to become wiser about immoral temptation and develop some specific strategies to strengthen my moral purity.

This is a book about developing strategies to build character, not an analysis of any particular sin. But part of developing moral purity is understanding how immoral temptation seduces and subdues. Wisdom about moral issues includes insight into the process of moral failure. Learning about that process is a vital part of developing moral fiber and moral values that last a lifetime and build a leader's legacy.

There is nothing that damages a leader's effectiveness and legacy more than moral failure. So, be wise about how it happens, what it will cost you, and what you can do to prevent it.

What Immorality Looks Like

In the book of Proverbs, personification is a literary device used to explain important concepts. Positive concepts such as wisdom are portrayed by personifying wisdom as a woman and revealing its characteristics through her words and practices. A negative use of this same literary device also portrays immorality as a woman. Two examples of this are in Proverbs 9:13–18 and 5:1–14. Analyzing immorality, personified through the actions of a woman named "Folly," will help you discern and resist immoral temptation.

Immoral Temptation Is Pervasive

Folly sits "by the doorway of her house, on a seat at the highest point of the city" (Prov. 9:14), calling out to all who pass by to come in for a visit. Immoral temptation is aggressively, publicly seeking ministry leaders who will give in to it. Certainly anyone with any sense of awareness can see how blatant this is in our culture. Immorality is no longer restrained by public decency. The temptation to be immoral is now continually in front of our eyes—on television, movies, bookstands, and the Internet.

Recently, my youngest son purchased a program at a professional sporting event. When he turned the program over, the photo on the back was of a mostly nude female dancer with three discreet patches covering just enough to keep her from being arrested. The advertisement was for a nude dancing club, sold to anyone with three dollars to buy the program. Immorality is calling out, publicly, openly, more brazenly than ever before in places where even children can be desensitized and made pliable to future temptation.

For ministry leaders, the computer has become the most public (and at the same time private) source of sexually immoral material and temptation. There are billions of electronic images, videos, and products available. Many ministry organizations have filters to help screen these sources, but no filter gets them all. Every screening process can be bypassed by simply using a public library computer. Learning to manage your e-mail and Internet access is essential to resisting the most accessible form of immoral temptation ever invented.

One young pastor got involved counseling a woman in an Internet chat room. Just trolling through that environment without supervision and accountability is a disaster waiting to happen. And disaster happened! After several weeks of daily "counseling," he "felt the Lord leading" him to fly across the country to meet with her in person. Two days of intensive "therapy" produced a predictable result. He called his wife and told her he was starting a new life with his counselee turned mistress.

This situation is tragic, yet absurd. He left his home, two children, and an attractive, well-educated, well-liked pastor's wife for a divorcee with two children living in a daily rental motel. And to top it off, the other woman's husband was still hovering in the picture and the pastor started "counseling" him as well. What a bizarre mess!

Immoral Temptation Is Aggressive

Folly calls out "to those who pass by, who go straight ahead on their paths" (Prov. 9:15). There was a time in the not-too-distant past when immorality was available but you had to know where to get it. Now, like never before, it comes looking for you. It will track you down while you are on a "straight path" with no intention of being tempted or enticed.

Television astounds me with its insidious ability to incorporate sexual immorality into almost any show. Over and over, our family has been enjoying some program when sexual immorality is introduced (always in a positive light). Recently, we were watching a sitcom about a married couple (sounds safe, right?). The couple was recounting their early years and of course had to go into great detail (accompanied by the laugh track) about their fornication prior to marriage. Of course, "fornication" was never mentioned—just the bliss of premarital sex and how much it supposedly strengthened their marriage. Never mind the truth. Premarital sex does not improve marriage relationships. Not in real life. Never.

Good thing this was fiction! Otherwise, it would have strained every level of credibility. But tragic lies were delivered to our children in an amusing, seemingly factual way. The message—sex outside of marriage is good—weaseled itself into our home right under our noses.

A few years ago, the movie *Titanic* did the same thing. Fascinated by the story and the sound track, my wife and I went to see this PG-13-rated movie, hoping to take our children later. Frontal nudity of the leading lady, not a passing shot but a pose for a painting, was a centerpiece (or centerfold) for the film. My anger boiled over that night! Once again, the tempting message of sexual immorality aggressively attacked us under the guise of a tragic love story. Millions of American teenage girls saw this movie and learned its lesson—meet a guy and strip if you want him to like you.

Your computer, even if you do not seek pornography, can still be a problem. Pornographers
are not waiting passively for you to find them. My
computer regularly receives unsolicited e-mail con-
taining pornography or links to pornographic web
sites. Most of the time, filters intercept these messages. But occasionally, one slips through and gets
opened.

Be careful how you handle these images. One
pastor opened this kind of e-mail only to have his
secretary walk into his office at just that moment.
Rather than explaining what had happened and
accounting for the decision, they agreed to cover it
up. Predictably, that did not work. Within weeks,
the issue had boiled into a major church controversy that ultimately cost him his pastorate.

If you feel like you are under attack, you are.
The temptation to be sexually immoral is aggressively pursuing you!

Immoral Temptation Overpromises and Underdelivers

Good salespeople avoid the ego-driven mistake of overpromising and underdelivering. They
do just the opposite. Folly makes this mistake over
and over. She promises that immorality will deliver
the opposite of its true results. She appeals to the
"inexperienced" to come in for a visit and to the
"one who lacks sense" (Prov. 9:16) to share her

secret wisdom. Sexual immorality promises pleasure, satisfaction, and fulfillment it does not and cannot produce. But that does not stop it from making outrageous claims and promises. Sadly, it doesn't stop ministry leaders from gullibly falling for its lies.

A friend of mine left his wife for another woman. He told me about his mistress, "When I'm with her, I am truly alive. She understands me like no one else. We connect on a level that I have never experienced before." But two years later, after he had divorced his wife, damaged his relationship with his children, and lost his business (and was not able to get a job), he was singing a different tune.

"I can't believe I did it," he told me. He had succumbed to the siren song of immorality. He really believed his new relationship would take him places he had never been before. He was right—but he did not know those places included the unemployment office and the food stamp line. His "depth of insight" turned into the deep end of the pool.

Immorality promises so much. In the early days of every immoral relationship there is the heady rush of infatuation and the raw pleasure of unleashed sexual energy. New awareness, new sharpness, supposedly new insight seems to be exploding. But it is false insight and false hope—a sham perpetuated on the unwise. Immorality promises the moon and stars, but it delivers destruction and death.

What Immorality Will Do to You

Continuing the personification of immorality in Proverbs, the results of immorality are portrayed in Proverbs 5:1–14. The life-shattering results are devastating. Here is how the Bible describes some of those results.

Leaves You Bitter, Broken, and Alone

The results of immorality are "as bitter as wormwood" and as "sharp as a double-edged sword" (Prov. 5:4). An immoral relationship begins with an emotional rush. Like a sugar-high, it does not last. A pastor who left his wife for another woman learned this lesson. When his mistress left him for another man, he was bitter ("How could she do this to me?") and alone. He wound up living in a one-room, fleabag hotel in a rough part of town while he looked for a minimum wage job.

Years later, when he told me his story, his primary memory was how alone he felt. He felt separated from God, his family, his church, and, in a sense, even himself. He felt so distant from the person he used to be and wanted to be. He remembered lying awake at night and wondering if anyone even cared if he were alive. A business leader who committed adultery and moved in with his lover told me his greatest loss was the respect of and relationship with his children. They completely cut him off!

Immorality entices you with Technicolor promises of emotional intimacy, but usually leaves you bitter and alone. You lose your family, your church, your livelihood, your friends, and even yourself. You will be alone, and lonely—which can be a suicidal combination.

Steals Your Strength and Makes You Sick

When you are immoral, you give "your vitality to others" and "your years to someone cruel" (Prov. 5:9) while "your physical body [is] consumed" (Prov. 5:11). A woman, a "kept woman" as she described herself, waited for two decades for her paramour to leave his wife and marry her. One day, when the long-term affair was finally revealed, the man chose to stay with his wife and rebuild his marriage. What a disaster for the mistress! She had given the best years of her life to an immoral relationship, believing it would ultimately bring her happiness.

Another man confessed an immoral relationship with some relief. He told me how taxing it had been to maintain two women financially. Only a fool would attempt what he had done for years! Now, he was facing a major health crisis brought on by stress and overwork. He had literally sacrificed his health to sustain his immoral lifestyle.

The most tragic possible result, however, is getting a sexually transmitted disease—particularly

AIDS. Can you imagine a more dastardly act than being sexually unfaithful to your spouse, getting a sexually transmitted disease, and then giving it to him or her (or even to an unborn child)? This is the most devastating physical result possible, yet it is not so far-fetched in our culture. Immorality can destroy you, literally, from the inside out.

Takes Your Money and Damages Your Lifestyle

An immoral lifestyle is expensive. The Bible warns "strangers will drain your resources, and your earnings will end up in a foreigner's house" (Prov. 5:10). Basically, immoral sex will cost you— big time!

Think of the ways immorality costs money. First, you have to pay the expenses for the mistress. One minister thought he had a foolproof plan for keeping his affair a secret. He had his mistress travel on the same itinerary when he was on the road and meet in his hotel room. While it kept the immoral relationship a secret for a long time, it also cost a boatload of money. Even if you do not go to that extreme, there are all the expenses that go with "dating"—gifts, meals, and the inevitable hotel rooms.

Second, you have to pay for the expenses of keeping your secret. One young minister bought a separate computer and maintained separate Internet accounts to hide his addiction to Internet pornography. He also had the added expense of long distance bills for phone sex and secret credit cards for sexually explicit materials he obtained. What started out costing a few dollars a month turned into thousands of dollars of expenses.

Third, you will pay for the damage your immorality does to others. You may have to pay for a divorce. Or your family may stay together, and you will get to pay for counseling for yourself, your spouse, and your children. You may be blackmailed and forced to pay money to keep others quiet about your sin. You may lose your job and take a severe pay cut with the temporary work you find to survive. You will probably have some damage to your health from the stress of the affair or perhaps from getting a sexually transmitted disease.

Anyway you look at it, immorality is expensive.

Maintaining Moral Purity

That's enough bad news. You get the picture! In fact, you probably know someone who has been immoral. That person's life illustrates some of the points made above. Perhaps you have been drifting toward succumbing to immoral temptation and these warnings have sobered you.

So, how do you keep from giving in to the pervasive temptations in our culture to be immoral? What can you do, positively and proactively, to keep yourself morally pure? And if you are already on the slippery slope toward moral failure, how can you find a sure foothold and start going in the other direction? Here are some specific suggestions to help you maintain moral purity.

Pour Energy into Your Marriage

Married sex is the best sexual relationship possible. The erotic way married sex is described in the Bible leaves no doubt that this is God's plan for sexual fulfillment. Song of Solomon is a good example. Another is the second part of Proverbs 5, in contrast to the first half of the chapter about immorality. Referring to sex in marriage the Bible says, "Drink water from your own cistern, water flowing from your own well. . . . Let your fountain be blessed and take pleasure in the wife of your youth. . . . [L]et her breasts always satisfy you; be lost in her love forever" (Prov. 5:15, 18, 19).

Wow! Clearly, God wants you to have a fulfilling sexual relationship in your marriage. What many couples in our sex-saturated society underestimate is how little they really know about sexual fulfillment when they get married and how much work it takes to develop a mutually satisfying, long-term sexual relationship.

Developing a fulfilling married sexual relationship, with one partner over a lifetime, takes work. You might be in a difficult situation in your marriage and be thinking, *If you only knew how impossible my wife [or husband] is on this subject.* But consider your options. You can work on your seemingly impossible situation—counseling, reading books, resolving differences, clarifying expectations—and it will cost you time, energy, and money. Or you can have an affair, get hooked on Internet pornography, or frequent strip clubs—and these will *really* cost you time, energy, and money.

But consider the outcomes. If you work on your married sexual fulfillment for a decade (yes, it might take that long) and it becomes fully satisfying, then you have years and years of guiltless pleasure ahead. If you look elsewhere for fulfillment, you know from reading this chapter what the cost will be. So, the choice is easy. Pour the energy into developing a healthy, mutually satisfying sexual relationship in your marriage.

The reluctance of men to invest in their marriage is amazing. Once, while sitting in a man's "gun room" surrounded by expensively mounted hunting trophies, the hunter told me, "Two hundred dollars is just too much money to spend on a marriage retreat." Unbelievable! He had guns that cost many times that much and dead heads staring down from the ceiling that exceeded that price. But the idea of spending money on improving his marriage was wasteful. Make the decision to invest in your marriage!

If you are not married, managing your sexuality also is difficult but possible. These next suggestions will help you, whether you are married or not, to pursue moral purity.

Limit Exposure to Immoral Influences

The temptation to be immoral is aggressively stalking you. You must take specific steps to protect yourself and your family from unlimited exposure to sexuality in our culture. Since it is pervasive, it is impossible to avoid it entirely. But you can take specific steps to limit the immoral influences that are trying to sway you.

Limit the amount and kind of television you watch. For the first year we were married, we chose not to have a television in our home. That helped us get control of it from the beginning of our marriage. We now own several televisions—but we monitor them and screen what we watch. We avoid any program that blatantly glorifies sexual immorality or any other contradiction of our values. We discuss more subtle influences and help our children analyze what they are watching. We turn off programs that surprise us with immoral content. We do not have access to any pay-per-view channels that show sexually explicit movies or programs.

Choose carefully the kind of movies you attend or videos you rent. This can be difficult to monitor but we made one very simple choice early in our marriage that has had profound, positive results. We do not view R-rated movies (*The Passion of the Christ* was our only exception). Making this choice may have caused us to miss a few good movies over the years. But it has also spared us seeing hundreds of big-screen sexual relationships that would have tempted us to immoral behavior and desensitized us to sexual fulfillment only in married sex.

Stay away from places that sell sex. God has some special ministers and missionaries who work with sex workers. These people have strict accountability standards and go to great lengths to maintain their moral purity. Thank God for their work! But most ministry leaders simply need to avoid strip clubs, nude bars, pornography stores, and other sexually explicit establishments.

Get control of your Internet use. Put filters on your computer and ask someone else to control the password. Use a program that automatically communicates every Web site you visit to an accountability partner. If necessary, take the drastic step of giving up the Internet at home and only using it on a public computer in your office.

Leaders who travel must take special care in these areas. If you struggle to control television viewing, have the hotel remove the television from your room upon arrival. If that is not possible, disconnect the power cord or cable connection and remove the cord from the room. When possible, do not travel alone. When you travel, plan how you will use your free time so that you are not tempted toward inappropriate activity.

Some of this may sound legalistic. No doubt, these are self-imposed, arbitrary rules. Legalism, however, is when one person imposes his or her standards on another person. Imposing these standards on yourself is not legalism; it's self-management. These standards are not requirements, unless you choose them to be. Therefore, they are not legalistic rules but wise, self-imposed limits that protect you from moments of weakness. A good friend has a desk plaque that says, "Others may, I cannot." Leaders adopt higher personal standards because their influence, for good or bad, exceeds that of others.

Unlimited, unscreened exposure to immorality in the culture desensitizes you. Like a persistent river, it erodes your moral convictions. Most people do not plunge into immorality; they drift into it. You can limit the drift by specific actions to limit your exposure to immoral influences.

Develop Accountability Relationships

Another aspect of maintaining purity is accountability to people who care about you, know you better than you know yourself, and are willing to confront you when you are wrong. Too many people think of accountability relationships as formal, sterile groups that meet to grill each other. While formal groups are helpful, other kinds of relationships can be just as motivating toward moral purity.

Two primary relationships that motivate my purity are my wife and children. Not disappointing my children has been a primary motivator to keep me morally right. Developing transparency with my wife and children has helped keep me morally straight.

For example, I am transparent with my wife about my whereabouts. She always knows where I am, whom I am with, and what I am doing. This requires very little effort on my part. Many days are routine, and she knows my routine. But if I go anywhere unusual, spend time with anyone (particularly women) who are not part of my routine, or do anything that might compromise my purity, I tell my wife immediately! My wife never wonders who I'm with or what I'm doing or where I am. She knows, and that accountability helps maintain my moral purity.

We also made an important decision about transparency with our children. Before our children were born, my wife and I decided we would never do anything for entertainment our children could not share. That does not mean we have not done things without our children! It simply means we do not go anywhere, watch anything, or read anything we would not want our children to know about (or later do if they were really interested). This one decision has kept me from many questionable activities and helped me maintain moral purity.

Purity is also maintained through transparency with a few close, same-sex friends. These friends can help you individually or as a formal group. Some might wonder about the same-sex aspect of accountability relationships. This is an absolute standard. While you may enjoy platonic or professional relationships with members of the opposite sex, only same-sex relationships should be developed as accountability relationships. True accountability relationships require a level of frankness not possible or appropriate in a relationship with someone of the opposite sex (other than your spouse).

These are not sexist comments, just practical observations. God values both sexes equally and wants both men and women to have meaningful accountability relationships. But, apart from your spouse, an accountability relationship sharing the details of your moral life, sexual practices, and responses to temptation is not appropriate with a person of the opposite sex.

Take Simple Steps to Protect Yourself

There are other simple things you can do to protect yourself from sexual temptation and from false accusations of immorality. Here are five simple things to do:

1. Put a window, with a shade, in your office door. When you are in your office alone, close the shade for privacy. When you are talking with anyone, man or woman, open the shade. This way, you can have privacy with the person but openness about your actions.

2. Counsel persons of the opposite sex carefully. Some pastors, for example, do not meet with or counsel women privately. While this is certainly a permissible standard, it is not practical for all pastors. If, as a male leader, you do counsel women, set up some ground rules. For example, you will only meet with a woman in your office while another person (like a secretary or staff member) is present in an outer office. You will only meet with a woman with your wife's full knowledge and permission. You may also want to set a fixed number of appointments you will have with any female counselee before referral.

3. Avoid hosting persons of the opposite sex socially or being alone with them in business or professional settings. For example, my work occasionally requires me to host a woman for a meal. My wife or assistant always accompanies me (or I simply do not go). The same is true when unexpected travel changes mean I must ride with or transport a woman (such as from the airport). When that happens, I call my wife or assistant and inform them of the details. I usually call them again when we arrive at our destination.

4. Give unlimited access to your computer and operate it in the open. I arrange my computer screen so that it can be seen from the door to my office. Anyone walking by can look in and see what I am doing. Key staff members know my password and have access to my computer. No secrets! My Internet use is tracked and can be analyzed at any time. Again, no secrets!

5. Avoid touching members of the opposite sex. Our family is a bunch of huggers! I am naturally gregarious. I like to touch, hug, and pat people. But the risk of being misinterpreted, misunderstood, and possibly communicating a wrong message means touching opposite sex coworkers is off limits. This may seem like a rigid standard, especially for the naturally friendly, but it is a necessary standard.

What If It's Too Late?

Perhaps you are already involved in immoral behavior. You are having an affair, involved in pornography, or dabbling with homosexual or incestuous behavior. You want out! What should you do?

You must be completely honest. Choose a trusted confidant, a wise leader, who can help you through the process of confession and restoration, and tell him everything.

You must confess your sin and bear your consequences. Those consequences will probably mean that you will lose your ministry leadership role. You may lose your job and paycheck. Your family, and others involved in your sin, will be hurt. But delaying the inevitable will only make the situation more painful and the consequences more intense.

Resist the temptation toward self-justification. What you are doing is your fault, period. It is astounding how many reasons are used to justify immoral behavior. It's your fault it happened, case closed! Stop blaming your wife, mother, church, children, the world, and the devil. You are immoral because you choose to be. Choose to stop!

Do all you can to repair the damage. Be prepared for this to take awhile. It is unrealistic to think you can confess this kind of sin, be forgiven, and move on quickly. That is denial in its rawest form. Restoration from moral failure takes time. Wounded people, wounded relationships, and wounded churches need time to heal.

Take heart—restoration is possible! Ministry leaders can be forgiven. Families can be healed. Depending on the scope of their actions, some ministry leaders can be restored to some leadership roles. But restoration takes years, not weeks or months. Leaders who have been restored worked through these four steps over a period of years. There are no shortcuts. The process can't be rushed.

To be restored from moral sin requires honesty, confession, willingness to take full responsibility, resistance to self-justification, and hard work to repair the damage and prevent future sin. You can be restored but you need to stop what you are doing *now* and go purposefully, intentionally, in a new direction. Do not wait! Time will not make it easier. Sooner or later your secret will be exposed. Take responsibility, do the right thing, and come forward willingly.

———◆———

Leaving a positive leadership legacy takes a lifetime of effective ministry buttressed by solid Christian character. Moral failure, more than any other character flaw, can undermine all you have done over a lifetime. Moral failure calls into question everything about your ministry. Your followers lose trust in your moral authority and then wonder about everything you taught them. Moral failure means everything is called into question. Moral failure leaves a legacy—a very negative one.

Don't let this happen to you. Take whatever steps necessary to build moral purity in your life. Avoid the tragic mistake of investing decades in leading effectively and then destroying it with illicit pleasure. Stand for moral purity and take whatever steps necessary to protect your commitment so it lasts a lifetime.

CHAPTER FIVE

Learning Humility

WRITING INSTRUCTIONS ABOUT learning humility seems like an obvious, even outrageous contradiction. "Hey, listen to me. I'm humble and I can teach you how to do it," sounds more like arrogance than humility. This dichotomy has made this chapter difficult to write. Yet, humility is a core quality of remarkable leaders and must be addressed.

Humility is not my strength. I am still on the humility learning curve, and one of the challenges is a lack of role models. There seem to be very few genuinely humble leaders. But fortunately, a few humble men and women have crossed my path. Much of what is in this chapter I have learned from them—and tried to copy—as I am seeking to develop this important character trait.

What Is Humility?

What Humility Is Not

Some Christians wrongly think humility is debasing themselves, putting themselves down, or talking about how inadequate they are. One man regularly rose during open microphone sharing in church to confess how inadequate he was and how he often failed God. Every Sunday evening, he recounted his shortcomings and how he was "humbly" learning spiritual insights from them. In reality, he was enjoying the attention his confession created. His confessions did not demonstrate humility. They put him in the spotlight so he could be praised for his supposed piety.

Another woman consistently sought counsel about her problems. She frequently called or dropped by my office to tell me about her failures. She openly ridiculed herself, poking fun at her appearance, intelligence, and features. What was she really doing? Calling out, "Notice me!" Her claims of lowliness were really a perverse form of self-promotion. What she thought demonstrated humility really showed her deep emotional insecurity and how much she craved attention (and attracted it to herself).

A pastor, elected to chair a denominational group, started every meeting or presentation with a disclaimer about "how unworthy he was to be there." While it may have been appropriate the first time, it became wearisome over time. What he really appeared to be doing was prolonging his time on stage, thus magnifying his position, not just simply doing his job.

These examples are all based on the faulty concept that humility is self-debasement. Somehow, by putting ourselves down in public (or in private) we think we make ourselves more humble. While you are biblically responsible to "humble yourself" (more about that later), these practices simply do not accomplish that purpose. In short, they just do not get the job done.

A Better Understanding

What then is humility? Humility is appropriate self-appraisal, seeing yourself as God sees you. Humility is adopting God's perspective on who you are and what you are assigned to do. It is the attitude that emerges from the spiritual discipline of thinking about yourself like God thinks of you. Humble leaders accept their God-assigned identity and mission. In short, they are comfortable with who God says they are.

John the Baptist is a good example of this. When asked, "What can you tell us about yourself?" (John 1:22), he did not hesitate to answer. He did not drop his head or scuff his toe. He simply answered the question. John said, "I am a voice of one crying in the wilderness: Make straight the way of the Lord" (John 1:23).

John later added, "He is the One coming after me, whose sandal strap I'm not worthy to untie" (John 1:27). Of course, he was speaking of Jesus, whom he had come to introduce. Yet, in spite of Jesus' greatness and John's smallness by comparison, John still owned both his identity and mission. Jesus' preeminence did not invalidate John's role in God's overall plan.

Humble leaders have a balanced view of how God sees them. True, you are a sinner, but you are also a saint. You can do nothing good apart from God's power, but you are also given spiritual gifts by God and expected to use them. You have a sinful bent that taints everything you do, but you are also enabled to do good works that really bless others. Humility is learning to live between these tensions. Humility is accepting the reality of who God says you are and living it daily.

Some leaders err to one extreme or the other. Some say, "I'm a child of the King so I should live like a prince or princess." In some sense that is true. But that kind of statement is often an excuse to support a hedonistic, materialistic lifestyle that contradicts the spirit and example of Jesus. Others say, "I'm just a sinner, saved by grace." That is also true unless it becomes an excuse for poor choices and continued irresponsible living. You are a child of God and a sinner saved by grace. Humility results when you successfully live with both poles exerting appropriate gravitational control of your behavior.

A Key Question

New Testament leaders struggled with these issues. Paul confronted the attitude of some apostles and other church leaders in 1 Corinthians 4. In the midst of his instructions, he asked a probing question related to leadership that, when answered correctly, produces humility. Paul asked, "What do you have that you didn't receive?" (1 Cor. 4:7).

Since my late teen years, 1 Corinthians 4:7 has been my "life verse." This haunting question is penetrating, soul-searching. Made personal, I ask, "What do I have that I did not receive?" The answer? Not one thing.

For example, my genetic talents and abilities are a gift from God. My ability to read and write resulted from the work of grade school teachers. My children are a gift from God and my wife. My ministry position is possible because someone had a vision for a seminary years ago and millions of Christians have given time, energy, and money to make it happen. My car was bought with money I earned, yes, but I could earn it because someone gave it to support our ministry and made it earnable! On and on I could go.

For years I have tried to find one answer to this question, "What do I have that I did not receive?" Every possible answer can be traced back to some source over which I had no control or input. This has led me to this conclusion and affirmation: My life is a result of what God and others have done for me. When you come to that conviction, you will have started on the journey toward humility.

My life is a result of what God has done for me. He has saved me, given me purpose, and called me into ministry. He has gifted me with spiritual gifts and natural talents. God has structured my circumstances to shape my character and remake me into the image of Jesus. He has given me ministry positions, some supernatural results, and many life-shaping opportunities. God has done a lot for me and you too!

My life is also a result of what other people have done for me. Teachers taught me to read, write, do math, and solve problems. Church members invited me into their lives as a preacher, counselor, and leader. Generous Christians have supported me, paid for my education, and provided a way for me to support my family. Friends have corrected and enemies have attacked—and both have shaped my character. People have done a lot for me and you too!

Leaders learn humility by asking, "What do I have that I did not receive?" and affirming that life is a result of what God and others do for us. Doing this enables you to own your strengths and acknowledge your weaknesses.

You can own or acknowledge your strengths without arrogance or pretended false humility. For example, I am a good preacher. I can write that, honestly but not arrogantly, because it is not a self-achieved skill. I am a good preacher because God hardwired me with natural gifts for public speaking, professors taught me skills and information required to build a preaching ministry, and two churches allowed me to learn to preach by practicing on them for more than a decade. I own or acknowledge this strength and recognize it as a gift from God and a result of the shaping of others. Denying this reality is denying God's gifting and the contribution of so many who have enriched my life. To deny it with some kind of fake piety or aw-shucks blushing is not humility. Affirming a personal strength in the appropriate context and with the right attitude is evidence of genuine humility.

You can also own your weaknesses and allow them to promote humility. I am not a patient person. Eliminating waiting is a primary life goal! This is a weakness because it makes me snappy, frustrated, mean-spirited, and grumpy. It makes me a controller and, on my worst days, a manipulator. Admitting these things has not been easy. For years, my goal was to camouflage this weakness.

Gradually, I learned the spiritual discipline and freedom of admitting weaknesses. The most interesting result is how people respond. When my goal was camouflage, people were intent on pointing out my shortcomings and confronting me about them. As I have become more honest, people have become less critical and more forgiving.

Camouflage is really a flashing beacon that draws attention to character flaws. Transparency about them becomes a window. People see through me and do not seem to see so much of me as they did when my goal was denial. That is a good thing. Being honest about who we are, including our weaknesses, leads to humility. Trying to cover up our shortcomings reveals our pride in who we wish we were and who we want others to think we are.

Humility Essentials for Leaders

Why is humility so important, and so difficult, for leaders? Humility is difficult because leaders are successful people. You probably became a leader in your current ministry because you were successful. If you are successful in your current role, you will probably be promoted to some expanded leadership opportunity. Success is the breeding ground for pride. That is why leaders are more susceptible to pride than followers are and why developing humility is both more difficult and more essential for leaders.

There are several biblical reasons why humility is particularly important for leaders. Here are a few to consider.

God Opposes the Proud

What leader wants God to oppose him or her? Not one! Peter wrote, "God resists the proud" (1 Pet. 5:5). That is strong language. The word *resists* means "to draw up in battle array." Do you remember the familiar scene in old Westerns when the Indians would ride up on a ridge in a menacing battle line? Dramatic music would create tension, settlers would circle the wagons, and a battle would be imminent. It was not very historically accurate, but it was certainly dramatic.

The word *resists* means God draws himself up in battle array. It means he marshals all his resources and brings them up to the battle line. He swells the ranks, fills out the companies, and intimidates you with his awesome presence. When you, as a leader, are operating in pride, God comes against you with all he has. You can circle your wagons if you want, but to no avail. Arrogance leads to destruction. Humility, on the other hand, leads to God giving grace. Peter continues, "God resists the proud, but gives grace to the humble" (1 Pet. 5:5).

God Exalts the Humble

As a leader, you probably have a strong ego. You want to succeed, and you probably want to be promoted. You want to make more money, have more influence, and impact more people. But be careful. The problem is not having ambition; it's how you fulfill it.

James wrote, "Humble yourselves before the Lord, and He will exalt you" (James 4:10). Our motto is often, "Do all I can, can all I get, sit on the can, and burn the rest before anyone else gets it." We easily get trapped in self-promotion, self-aggrandizement, and self-centeredness. We think it—whatever *it* is—all depends on us. You want to be exalted. After all, the Bible says God will exalt you. But you only have half the equation right.

God wants to exalt you. The problem is the path you choose. Doing all you can to get your name in lights is not God's plan. God's plan is for you to choose humility, and then he will exalt you. He will do it in his way, in his time, and to the degree appropriate for your character. When God exalts you, you will enjoy it because it will be a gift from him.

God Leads the Humble

Your most common prayer as a leader is probably, "Lord, give me wisdom." Your second most common prayer might be, "Lord, show me what to do." We constantly ask God for direction, to reveal his plans, to show us his timing, or otherwise direct our steps. Leaders are supposed to show the way. The problem is, we don't always know the way.

The stakes are high and will only become higher as your influence grows. Dozens, hundreds, thousands, or even millions of people may be impacted by your decisions. You must decide what to preach weekly, when to build a new facility, who to employ on your ministry staff, what new program to launch, what old program to stop (good luck!), where to plant a new church, which community is open to new mission efforts, and how to gather the money to do all this. All of these decisions, and a dozen more like them, depend on your ability to find God's direction.

While there are many factors in hearing from God, one crucial issue is humility. David wrote, "[The Lord] leads the humble in what is right and teaches them His way" (Ps. 25:9). Humility is essential to hearing from God and sensing his direction. Leaders must practice humility because they are uniquely responsible to hear from God on behalf of the people they lead.

God Empowers the Humble

You will not lead very long before you realize how little your power matters. To accomplish supernatural results requires supernatural power. True spiritual leaders long for God's power to be demonstrated through them.

Moses was described as "a very humble man, more so than any man on the face of the earth" (Num. 12:3). That description set the stage for a series of events demonstrating God's favor and power on him. Aaron and Miriam had been critical of Moses and God confronted them. He addressed them directly from a pillar of cloud, reminding them that he spoke to Moses "directly, openly, and not in riddles" (Num. 12:8). Then he cursed Miriam with a skin disease. When Aaron cried for mercy, Moses interceded and God relented, confining the disease to a seven-day duration.

Moses knew God and could access his power. Do you and can you? That is a measure of spiritual leadership—knowing God and accessing his power. Moses' humility was a prerequisite to God's power being available to him. As you practice humility, God's power will more easily move through you.

God's Presence Surrounds the Humble

Isaiah quoted God as asking, "Heaven is My throne, and earth is My footstool. What house could you possibly build for Me?" (Isa. 66:1). In other words, why do you think a special house will guarantee my presence? This Old Testament passage foreshadows an important New Testament reality.

God is not housed in things made by humans but in humans themselves.

Isaiah continued quoting God, "I will look favorably on this kind of person: one who is humble, submissive in spirit, and who trembles at My word" (v. 2). God delights in showing himself present in and through humble leaders.

Do you know anyone who has the aura of God's presence? When you are around that person, you sense something unique, something supernatural, something peaceful and awe-filled all at the same time. A crucial part of God surrounding you with his presence is developing humility. God would rather demonstrate his presence through a humble leader than through a thousand cathedrals we might build to house him.

God's message is crystal clear. Humility is essential for leaders. Now, the more pressing question, how do we learn humility? How can you structure your circumstances to develop humility? What can you do to intentionally develop this important trait?

Learning Humility

The most interesting aspect of learning humility is this. It is a choice *you* make. Over and over the Bible says, "Humble yourself" (for example, James 4:10; 1 Pet. 5:6). You are responsible to humble yourself. There must be, then, biblical and practical steps you can take to learn humility.

This runs counter to those who feel responsible to humble others. The Bible tells you to "honor one another" (Rom. 12:10 NIV) and "humble yourself." It never says, "humble one another" and "honor yourself." Some Christians are reluctant to give honor because they are afraid of puffing up another person, of contributing to their pride. A pastor's wife once told me, "I never compliment my husband's sermons because I don't want him to get a big head."

She was well-intentioned but wrong! We are responsible to honor others and express gratitude to and for them. We should appreciate and compliment character and accomplishments. How a person responds to a genuine, appropriate compliment is their problem, not yours. Another person once told me, only half jokingly, that her ministry was keeping other people humble. This woman could have claimed the spiritual gift of criticism motivated by a root of bitterness!

She was wrong about her "ministry." No Christian has the responsibility to keep others humble. Attempting this on another person produces humiliation, not humility. You can humiliate someone, but you cannot humble that person. Allowing a circumstance to be humbling is a personal choice. Intentionally creating those circumstances is how you humble yourself. Here are some specific suggestions, concrete things you can do to learn humility.

Pray

A primary way to learn humility is to pray. The act of intentionally setting aside time to pray reveals so many things about your heart. When you pray, you demonstrate an attitude of dependence on God. You communicate neediness. You acknowledge powerlessness. You reveal your priorities and admit your weaknesses. Prayer—not so much the words you say but what the act itself reveals—is a powerful contributor to developing and maintaining humility.

As part of learning humility through prayer, there are several other steps you can take. First, kneel when you pray. Kneeling is a sign of submission and subservience. When you kneel before God, you practice humility. Many leaders only pray on the fly—while driving, before meals, prior to meetings, and in worship services. Prayer that promotes humility requires an intentional choice, both of time and posture.

Second, kneel to pray in public. Occasionally, during a public invitation or altar call, kneel publicly. This is not because God will better hear your prayers but because you need to humble yourself. Kneeling before your followers is a humbling

experience. When you are in that posture, you are
not the all-knowing leader. You are demonstrating
your need for God.

Third, pray with people. Leaders often pray
for people and in front of people but do not often
pray with people. Praying with people means you
take time, usually in a small group, to cry out to
God for both your personal and ministry needs.
Something humbling happens when you, as the
leader, confess your needs to God in the hearing of
your followers.

Ask Others to Pray for You

More than a decade ago, I initiated a group of
supporters called "The Prayer Team." My reasons
were many. I needed spiritual support as I moved
into more visible leadership roles. I had experienced
the impact of brothers and sisters with the ministry
of intercession and wanted to draw on their power.
I believe in prayer, yet it is not one of my strengths.
I wanted some real prayer warriors on my side.

When I wrote a public appeal for intercessors
to contact me if they wanted to be on the team, an
interesting thing happened. About half of the initial respondents were people I had never met. One
example was Cal Poncho Sr. Mr. Poncho is a Native
American believer, in his eighties, who wrote asking to be on the prayer team. He wrote, "When I
saw the picture of your young family on the day

you became our leader, I committed to pray for you every day. I have been doing that for months. I would like to be on your prayer team."

Getting Mr. Poncho's hand-scrawled letter was a moving experience. He had never met me and yet was already praying for me daily. I was humbled by his example of selflessness. As other letters like his arrived, I was deeply moved by the willingness of so many to pray for my family. God reminded me who his real heroes are!

For more than ten years, I have kept the prayer team active. Each month, I write them a personal letter outlining the needs and opportunities facing our family. I also include an overview of my monthly schedule, including travel plans. The act of writing that monthly letter humbles me. It reminds me there are people who are truly selfless servants, who want no public recognition, and who pray because it is their ministry. It reminds me that my true source of spiritual strength is the Lord and the prayers of his saints. Writing it reminds me I am not self-sufficient. I depend on an anonymous army.

The prayer team, now about forty strong, prays for me consistently (most pray daily). Most of them will never write a book, speak at a conference, or have any public notoriety. But they know, and I know, the source of whatever spiritual power, success, and accomplishment I have. The prayer team, and their continuing contribution to me, humbles me. And yes, they prayed me through writing this book!

Develop a Teachable Spirit

My grandmother had an amusing habit. No matter what you told her, she would say, "I know it." She was not expressing arrogance or a know-it-all attitude. Like some people say, "You know?" to keep others talking, she said, "I know it." Our family often joked there was nothing, no matter how unusual, Grandmother did not already know!

That's funny when it's a quirky habit, but it's not so funny when it is your real life perspective. Some leaders develop the attitude that they know more than everyone else, are smarter than everyone else, and have all the answers. As a young pastor, I once told my wife, "I wish everyone would stop questioning me and just do what I say. We would make some mistakes but mostly we would make progress. I know I am right most of the time." After my wife revived from fainting at my arrogance, we had a rather heated conversation. That was not my best day!

Developing the discipline of being a lifelong learner fosters humility. An older, prominent African-American pastor once asked me to speak at a marriage conference at his church. At the pre-conference banquet, he said, "Brother pastor, I have a problem with my church leaders I would like to consult with you about." I thought, *You've got to be kidding.* I could not imagine I would have anything at all to contribute to the conversation!

After he rolled out the problem, I suggested a simple solution. "There's wisdom in that," he said. I considered it a miracle I had said anything that made any sense, much less might be called wise. The pastor had a teachable spirit. He sought a fresh perspective. He was humble enough to ask a young Anglo pastor for his input. I marveled at this humility.

Another pastor, a peer for many years, calls me occasionally to talk about major leadership decisions. He is an effective, successful pastor, yet he wants to learn from me. Again, God has used that example to humble me and remind me to be teachable.

You can measure your teach-ability by asking some simple questions. What is the name of the last personal development book you read before this one? When you go to a conference or convention, do you actually attend the sessions or just hang out in the hallway talking? Do you attend worship and Bible study when you are not preaching or teaching? Do you seek advice from trusted colleagues prior to making major ministry decisions?

You can learn humility by asking others to teach you and taking concrete steps to continually learn from others.

Give Others the Credit

Another leadership discipline that deepens humility is developing the habit of making others successful and giving away the credit. For example, when your church grows, celebrate the Sunday school workers or the evangelism teams. When your staff accomplishes some significant project, bless them with public praise. If a mission team has unusual victories, allow the team members to get the credit. When you report to your board, give credit for successful projects to staff members who played an integral role.

Giving away the credit, even when some of it is rightly yours, is a specific way to learn humility. You are choosing to magnify others. Often, on the way home from such an experience I have prayed, "Thank you, Lord, for letting me bless a coworker. You know what I did on this project, and Lord, that's enough."

Part of this is also doing quiet things to make other people successful. A group of administrative assistants, a true high-performance team, modeled this principle. These women had one motto, "We get the work done." They did not fight over turf, did not argue about workload, did not gripe about how much had to be done, or otherwise pick at each other. Neither did they make a show of how they worked together. They simply, quietly, did whatever was necessary to make each other and their organization successful. They modeled humility. I learned from them an important principle. Humble workers make each other successful. They get the work done and do not care who gets the credit.

Develop the Discipline of Being Grateful

My wife and young children went round and round about thank-you notes. Ann insisted they be written. The children considered it an onerous task, but my wife is tenacious! She was determined her children would learn the discipline of being thankful. One way to do that is acknowledging gifts.

The root of the rebellion, both for my children when they were young and for ungrateful leaders, is the arrogant assumption that we deserve nice things people do for us. You assume you deserve a nice office, a generous salary, appreciation on your anniversary, respect from your staff, understanding from your supervisor, praise from your personnel committee, special treatment by your board, a full benefits plan, and an expense account.

You may think you deserve all this, but you do not. You don't deserve any of it. And if you have any of these things, your attitude toward them is vital. Your attitude should be gratitude for these good things God has allowed you to have as a leader. Christian leaders around the world have very few of these perks expected by American church leaders. Our attitude toward these blessings must be gratitude, not a sense of entitlement.

The discipline of being grateful is not primarily about writing thank-you notes. That is impractical for most of the blessings leaders enjoy. The issue is attitude. Gratitude, not entitlement, must be our perspective on the good things in our lives. Gratitude is rooted in and fosters deeper humility. Gratitude says, "Thank you, God. While I enjoy this, I don't deserve it." Entitlement says, "Come on people, is this the best you can do?" The discipline of being grateful is essential to learning humility.

————◆————

Learning humility is a spiritual challenge and a personal challenge. No one can do it for you. You must humble *yourself.* Choosing circumstances that intentionally redirect the spotlight from you as a leader toward God and others will be difficult. But your leadership legacy—the real spiritual impact you will make over a lifetime—depends on it. Find practical ways to humble yourself, and, slowly but surely, humility will emerge as a core leadership quality in your life.

CHAPTER SIX

Developing Servanthood

ALL CHRISTIAN LEADERS are servants, aren't they? They serve God. They serve people. They are often called "minister," which means "servant." Unfortunately, it's not that simple. Most of us started with the best intentions. We would always be servants—of the Lord and his people! But while we started as servants, we may have drifted. We can slowly, incrementally, develop expectations of being served rather than sacrificing ourselves for others.

To counter this drift, Christian leaders are often challenged to be servant leaders. The phrase "servant leadership" has been coined to describe an appropriate style for Christian leaders. While this terminology has much to offer, my introduction to it was problematic. My initial confusion set me on course to discover and define the essence of servant leadership.

Servant leadership was first presented to me as hands-on, pastoral care being the only model of true Christian ministry. Servant leaders, I was told, sacrifice themselves, care deeply and directly for people, shun position and recognition, and humble themselves at every opportunity. Servant leaders, according to this model, care for people in passionate and direct ways, taking every opportunity to emulate the personal ministry of Jesus.

Conversely, pastors or other leaders with a more executive or administrative style were denigrated for their aloofness and lack of concern. They were not servant leaders because they did not regularly get their hands dirty with the daily demands of ministering personally to people. This model did not seem to allow for other executive leaders—ministerial or corporate—to be servant leaders.

As I heard this explanation, much of it sounded good. Leaders *should* sacrifice themselves, shun recognition, care for people, and be personally involved with their followers. But is that the only model of leadership that can be called "servant leadership"? And beyond these concerns, how much of this behavior is required before a person is a true "servant leader"?

While listening to this presentation, my eye wandered to a scene outside the classroom window. A school employee was organizing some other employees for a landscaping project. Certainly this must be servant leadership! It was hands-on, dirty work, meeting the practical needs of a Christian institution. Little pay and almost no recognition would result.

Then I thought of the school president down the hall. Was it possible he was also a servant leader? Not by the definition I was hearing. He had a prominent position, much recognition, little contact with students, made a generous salary, seldom got his hands very dirty, and did almost nothing directly. An office full of staff carried out his directives! This tension bothered me. Something was askew. If the chief leader of a school training people for ministry could not be a servant leader, then what was the point?

So, I concluded that the definition and description I was hearing were inadequate. At that time, though, I did not have a better understanding. Now I do. Here is a more balanced model of servant leadership and some action plans to develop the character quality of servanthood as a leader.

Describing Servant Leadership

Servant leadership is, in its essence, an *attitude.* Servant leadership is defined more by who you are than by what you do. All servant leaders do not look alike, think alike, or minister alike. Defining servant leadership by any performance category or job description needlessly limits the possibilities.

Trying to comprehensively describe this process led me to this summary of where servant leadership originates, what gives it different forms, and what results. My process model for understanding servant leadership is:

Servant leadership happens when—
- a proper ministry motive is
- expressed through your personal mission,
- shaped by your individual attributes, and
- applied in your assigned ministry setting.

Let's walk through the four components of the model for servant leadership and some suggestions about how you can analyze and implement each part. Grasping the full picture of how this all fits together will help you have a healthier understanding of how you, whatever your leadership role, can become a servant leader and model servant leadership.

Get the Proper Ministry Motive

What drives you as a leader? What gets you out of bed in the morning, lights your fire, kicks you in the pants, makes your heart race, keeps you going when you're tired, and makes you hang in when you want to quit? In short, what motivates your ministry?

There are some bad, albeit common motives. Guilt is one. No matter how good your mother was at piling it on, guilt is a bad motive. Leaders who run on guilt are driven by an inner need that simply cannot be satisfied through service. This is really false guilt. Another word for this is *condemnation.* Since, "no condemnation now exists for those in Christ Jesus" (Rom. 8:1), false guilt simply cannot be a sustaining motive for ministry. Real guilt will not work either. True guilt results from conviction of sin and motivates repentance, not ministry to others.

Duty is another bad motive. You may do your duty for awhile, but sooner or later you will go AWOL. Leaders driven by duty are often trying to please someone who cannot be satisfied. For example, one leader was driven to succeed in ministry because he had promised his mother he would do it. She had long since died! This leader burned out trying to do his duty and fulfill a deathbed promise.

Money seems like a good motivator, but it's not. Many highly motivated people work in occupations (such as teaching and counseling) with limited salaries. One minister's father condemned him for entering ministry because it was not a lucrative profession. So, he spent the next two decades trying to make as much money as possible in ministry (and with other get-rich-quick ventures) to prove his father wrong. Money motivated him but undermined his effectiveness as a leader.

So, if guilt, duty, and money are poor motives, what is the best motive for ministry? The Bible is clear—love for God. Jesus said, "Love the Lord your God with all your heart, with all your soul, and with all your mind. This is the greatest and most important commandment" (Matt. 22:37–38). Jesus' audience for this pronouncement was significant. He was answering a question posed by the Pharisees. The Pharisees were prominent religious leaders at that time. Many were consummate legalists and elitists who understood the power of guilt, duty, and money. They often exploited people using these improper motives.

Jesus told these religious elitists that loving God was the first commandment, the greatest good, and the highest priority. Nothing about this has changed over the past two millennia. Jesus says the same thing to you. Love for God must be the driving force motivating your ministry.

Closely connected with loving God is loving people. Jesus also told the Pharisees that the second commandment was to love their neighbor. He said, "The second [commandment] is like it: Love your neighbor as yourself" (Matt. 22:39). This was a startling revelation! The Pharisees enjoyed the prestige of membership in an elite class. They would not normally acknowledge their neighbor, unless it was another Pharisee. They certainly would not consider a lower class person an object of love. Yet, Jesus was clear. Love God. Love people. That sums it all up!

On another occasion (Mark 10:35–45), Jesus described Christian leadership and contrasted it with worldly models. Two disciples, James and John, asked if they could "sit at Your [Jesus'] right hand and at Your left in Your glory." Jesus challenged them, in essence saying, "You don't know what you are asking." They insisted they did!

Jesus then used the occasion to teach on the stark contrast between worldly and Christian leadership styles. He called them to a new way of leading: "Whoever wants to become great among you must be your servant, and whoever wants to be first among you must be a slave to all" (Mark 10:43–44). Christian leaders are servants who enslave themselves for the good of their followers. Like Jesus, Christian leaders are called to sacrifice themselves—even giving their lives—like our model leader Jesus.

Clearly, a servant attitude is essential for effective Christian leadership. Christian leadership and worldly leadership are markedly different. They are not the same, never have been the same, and stand in stark contrast to each other. The struggles in this passage for the Christian leader are attitudinal. Jesus evaluates leaders by their attitude and the results that emerge (not the other way around).

This is also seen in the foot washing story in John 13:1–11. Jesus offered to wash Peter's feet, and predictably, Peter refused. But when Jesus said, "If

I don't wash you, you have no part with Me," Peter changed his mind! Jesus then explained that it wasn't a bath Peter needed but an attitude change about service. His arrogance was blocking his ability to receive service and ultimately to lead as a servant.

Peter probably had his feet washed every day, or at least on many days, by a servant. So the act of foot washing was not that unusual. The Person who was washing Peter's feet, not the act, was what was troubling Peter. Jesus' attitude made this more than a grandstanding ritual. Paul wrote, "Make your own attitude that of Christ Jesus" (Phil. 2:5). Jesus' servant attitude prompted him to wash feet and ultimately go to the cross. We are admonished to have the same attitude as Jesus.

Our attitude and demeanor create an unseen but very real aroma around our actions. The fragrance we want to emanate is the aroma of Jesus (2 Cor. 2:15). This aura surrounding our actions comes from our motives. People can sniff out selfish, self-serving, self-absorbed motives. No matter how you dress them up or cover them up, your true motives will be revealed. The driving motive for servant leaders, for truly Christian leaders, must be love—love for God and love for others.

Clarify Your Personal Mission

Many leaders have a written mission statement that drives their organization. We understand the power of corporate statements like these. But many leaders do not apply this principle on a personal basis. They do not have a personal mission statement. Do you?

A personal mission statement is a one-sentence statement of God's unique assignment for you. Jesus' personal mission was "to seek and to save the lost" (Luke 19:10). Paul summarized his mission by claiming "I have become its [the church's] minister . . . so that we may present everyone mature in Christ" (Col. 1:25, 28). My personal mission statement is "God has called and equipped me to provide visionary leadership and train others to be effective leaders."

Why is it important to define your personal mission in the context of becoming a servant leader? Your personal mission puts limits on your ministry. One of the hardest lessons to learn is some opportunities should be declined. When you do not do this, you feel frustrated and angry. When you lead within the limits of your personal mission, your motives and attitude will usually be good. You will serve more easily and effectively.

Your personal mission also gives you a sense of security. You know you are pleasing God so you can relax. You are not trying to please people and are not stressed by demands you cannot meet. You have a sense of purpose and intentionality. You know you are working from your strengths.

You will enjoy more frequent success that inspires further service.

Even though you may feel successful, it comes with a sense of humility. You know you are doing what God made you to do! You are profoundly grateful to God for calling you, equipping you, and giving you the opportunity to serve him. You have received his mission assignment so you know you are an integral part of his work. Focusing on your personal mission helps alleviate jealousy and competition in ministry. You know your mission and by implication know others have different missions. You are not competing with anyone. Your only competition is with your own God-produced personal standards, expectations, and potentialities.

Writing a personal mission statement is more than an exercise in personalized corporate planning. It must be a spiritual process. Begin by studying the Bible. Discover the missions of biblical characters. Study the theology of the Kingdom. Understand God's mission in the world. Allow God to steep these insights into your mind before you write your statement. Remember, as a Christian leader, your mission is a reflection and extension of God's mission in the world.

Next, ask friends and family members for their evaluation and insight. Ask others to appraise your strengths, weaknesses, liabilities, gifts, and talents. Listen also to casual comments, even from your critics. Sometimes a critic may say the right thing in the wrong way but the core insight within the criticism is helpful. Also, be careful not to ignore your promoters, allowing false humility to keep you from owning your strengths. Friends who know you well can help you discern and celebrate how God plans to use you. Part of learning from others might also be using formal testing to discover your spiritual gifts, leadership style, relational style, or learning abilities.

Another important source for developing your personal mission statement is reflecting on your life and ministry experiences. Ask yourself questions such as:

- What do I really enjoy?
- What am I really good at?
- What does God bless when I do it?
- What is really special or unique about me?
- What am I doing that is not very productive?

As you study the Bible, talk with others, and reflect on your experience through meditative prayer, some ideas will emerge. Write them down! Writing has a remarkable way of crystallizing our thoughts. Write your ideas, share them with a few key people, ask for reflection, and continue to sharpen and polish. Try to keep it to one short sentence. Resist the temptation to make it a flowery thesis rather than a laser sharp, precise statement.

Remember, there is no good writing—only good rewriting.

Depending on your age and stage of leadership, you may need to redo this process often. Having walked dozens of leaders through this process, the following frequency seems helpful, although by no means absolute:

1. Redo this process every year in your twenties.
2. Redo this process every two to three years in your thirties.
3. Redo this process twice in your forties.
4. Redo this process once each decade after that.

Writing your personal mission statement will be a liberating experience. Keep your statement flexible and adjust it over time. Do not worry about getting it exactly right by some artificial standard. Develop a working draft and use it for awhile. Adjust it as needed. Do not worry if others do not fully understand its meaning. Just be sure you do, and let it guide you toward greater effectiveness.

Understand Your Individual Attributes

Servant leaders with the right motive and a clear mission are still not all alike. There are at least seven different aspects of who we are that impact how we serve. These include personality, gifts, abilities, calling, training, experiences, and character.

There is incredible variety within each of these categories. Personality types have different classifications depending on the system used. Different popular writers/speakers use terminology such as type A or type B; lions, otters, beavers, or retrievers; sanguine, choleric, melancholy, or phlegmatic; and so on. You probably fit one or more of these categories. But be careful about limiting yourself by these descriptions. Personality cannot be quantified. You are a one-of-a-kind creation. Celebrate that!

Different leaders also have different spiritual and natural gifts. There are various lists of spiritual gifts in the Bible and multiple ways to explain and understand their distribution and use among believers. Most leaders also have natural gifts—talents God simply wired them with genetically. Possible combinations of spiritual and natural gifts are too diverse to attempt to categorize. Leaders are gifted people. You have a unique gift-mix concocted by God. Celebrate that as well!

Leaders have different levels of training, education, and skill development. Life experiences vary. Learning opportunities, formal and informal, are widely varied among leaders. Character development also happens uniquely over a lifetime. Learned skill sets become obsolete and new skills must be mastered.

In short, there is infinite variety within these seven categories. Leaders are unique and distinct

in their personality, gifts, abilities, calling, training, experiences, and character. Every person is a
pick-and-choose combination, created by God and
shaped by circumstances he allows. The good news
is God likes variety. Consider how many different
kinds of flowers there are in the world. If God likes
variety among flowers, certainly he must enjoy it
among his leaders.

My youngest son has been trying to solve the
problem of how many different bracket results are
possible in the annual NCAA National Basketball
Tournament—"March Madness." He has been
trying to determine how many different potential
brackets could result depending on all the possible
single-game outcomes! I'm sure there is an answer,
but it's beyond me. I will settle for infinite!

When you consider all the different ways these
seven categories of individual attributes combine
and relate, it's like trying to solve the bracket problem. There are so many variables it is impossible to
settle on one standard model of what a leader must
be like.

This is a good thing! We are not all supposed
to be alike. Being a servant leader is not copying
anyone else. It's not about emulating anyone else's
model. No one collection or arrangement creates
the model servant leader. Being a servant leader
means you are motivated by love to live out your
mission through your unique constellation of per-

sonal attributes from these seven categories. You are, and should be, one of a kind.

Work in Your Ministry Setting

Every leader also has been assigned a unique ministry setting. These also have multiple variables—geographic, cultural, social, economic, and spiritual settings. No two places are alike. Everyone works in a unique setting. The only thing all ministry settings seem to have in common is they are all hard!

Servant leadership will take different forms according to the setting. For example, servant leadership in a country club community will be different from that in a homeless shelter. But servant leadership is possible in both settings. Servant leadership also looks different in distinct cultural settings. What demonstrates humility in a Korean church might communicate arrogance in a Hispanic community. African-American pastors have a very different leadership style from that of Japanese pastors. Cultural and geographic factors matter in defining an appropriate leadership style.

Ministry setting is often overlooked in defining leadership style. Young pastors sometimes make this mistake when learning from older pastors or pastors of larger churches. The pastor who shaped me had been a pastor for about twenty-five years, mostly in one church. I observed him and tried to lead the same way when I became a pastor.

What a disaster! He was in a much larger church, had long tenure, had earned much respect and trust, was in a different community, and had a different constituency. Nonetheless, he was my model so I copied him. The results? I alienated many people. Why? I did not understand the dynamics producing his leadership style. I simply copied it without regard for my ministry setting.

Some young leaders also make another common mistake. They attend a conference hosted by a large church in a different setting and then try to implement what they learn without filtering it into their context. What is taught and learned is valid, but without proper interpretation it can be toxic. Principles always supersede programs and practices. Servant leaders understand this. They recognize that situational leadership (not situational ethics) is valid. A servant leader does things differently depending on the ministry situation and setting.

Servant leadership happens when a proper ministry motive is expressed through your personal mission, shaped by your individual attributes, and applied in your assigned ministry setting. Servant leadership takes many legitimate forms and has many different expressions. But the issue, the key issue, is motive. The aroma surrounding our actions— the unmistakable aroma of Jesus Christ—is what marks real servant leaders. Do not concentrate on your role or ministry results to determine if you are a servant leader. Look at your heart.

Shaping Love as Your Motive

Since motive is the crucial issue for servant leaders, it deserves additional consideration. Some people think motive just happens. It does not. You can take specific actions to shape your motives as a leader. You can choose to serve others, sense the purity of your motive in those moments, and draw on that resource in other leadership settings. While motives are difficult to describe or define, they are not difficult to discern! Followers have an innate sense of the true motives of their leaders.

Most assume motive is a spiritual reality that cannot be quantified or shaped. Motives are important, yet difficult to understand. Since understanding them is so hard, shaping them must be even more challenging. But that is not the case. Simple service situations can be structured that will help purify your motives. Here are some choices you can make to shape your motives.

Choose to do a dirty job. Most leaders are not expected to do dirty work—like cleaning toilets, changing diapers, or mowing the lawn. Frankly, most of the time leaders should not do these jobs. Good leaders recruit, employ, and empower people to do all kinds of things like this. Part of being a good leader is realizing how different people can make a meaningful contribution and utilizing them appropriately.

But one way to do a "motive check" is to choose a dirty job and do it. One church leader, struggling with his motives, contacted his pastor and said, "The next time you have a really dirty job—like a toilet backed up or something—call me." Within days, plumbing that always worked backed up badly! The opportunity to do some really dirty work presented itself, and with it came a cleansing of both a bathroom and a young businessman's heart. Choosing to do a job normally beneath this store manager's dignity humbled him and helped him reconnect to love as a motive for ministry.

Doing something like cleaning up a sewage problem, without any fanfare or expectation of appreciation, can humble you. It demonstrates that you are not above doing anything required of your followers. It sharpens your motives. There is no glamour, just the satisfaction of knowing you are willing to serve. There are no accolades, just the satisfaction of emulating Jesus.

Choose to serve anonymously. A second scenario that sharpens motive is choosing to do something anonymously. I was once responsible for a prolonged volunteer building project. For about two years, I spent every holiday weekend helping build a major ministry facility. Each time I worked with a different set of volunteers. Most did not know I was the CEO of the organization building the facility. I always tried to join a work crew, keep my identity quiet, and grind out the work.

One day, while moving multiple piles of plywood into position for decking, my coworker asked, "What do you do for a living?" When I told him, he replied, "Wow, and you're out here *working?*" My cover was blown!

But while it lasted, it was a great opportunity to work without recognition. I served anonymously, usually doing basic work setting the stage for the real craftsmen who would return on Monday. Their work was what people would see. They would get the well-deserved credit. Each session left me sore, yet deeply satisfied with what I had done. I had worked hard because of love—for the Lord, his work, and for the building's ultimate purpose and mission. I had worked anonymously without recognition or reward other than purified motives. It felt good and reminded me that all my work should be done with this spirit.

Choose to serve secretly. Occasionally, opportunities arise when leaders can serve without ever revealing their involvement. Serving secretly, perhaps like nothing else, will deepen love as your leadership motive.

For example, you can give money to meet a need only you know about. Give cash directly to the person, secretly and anonymously. You can make another person successful without him knowing of your influence. You can meet a personal need without anyone knowing you have been involved. You can solve a problem without revealing yourself as the solution. Personal examples, on this point, have to remain secret. If I wrote about them, some of their power to shape my motives would be lost!

When I first became a denominational leader, my predecessor told me, "The things you will do in this job that will mean the most to you, no one else will ever know about." He was absolutely right! My most deeply satisfying ministry has not been public ministry. It has been ministry done quietly, often secretly. Doing meaningful things for others, with only God for an audience, is a unique pleasure.

The recipient of secret service can also learn something about motives for ministry leadership. When our first child was born, a major department store delivered a full bedroom suite of furniture to our home. At first we refused delivery, denying we had made such an order. Then we realized we were the recipient of someone's secret service. Many years later, we still don't know who gave us the gift. We learned a powerful lesson. Someone loved us enough to serve us without any reward. Servant leaders do the same thing for others.

Choose to serve an enemy. Jesus said, "Love your enemies" (Matt. 5:44). Since he did not give pointless instructions, Jesus' admonition means you will have some enemies to love! Leading involves taking public positions, making controversial decisions, and having opinions or perspectives others do not share. This creates opponents and critics who can become enemies. One way to learn to love others is to choose to serve an enemy.

Once, another leader asked me to help him with a family crisis. He had been a vocal, public critic of my ministry. Coming to me was humbling for him. Instead of referring him for help, I decided to help him personally and quietly. God used the circumstances to remind me how to love someone, no matter how he had treated me, and deepened love as my motive for ministry.

Pastors often have the opportunity to love critics and serve them quietly. On several occasions, church members have been critical of me or opposed my leadership and very soon after had a personal or family crisis. Something spiritually profound happens when you provide pastoral care for someone who does not care much for you. More than ministry occurs. God is often giving you a major motive check and the opportunity to sharpen your love for him and his people.

Choose to make someone else successful. A unique dynamic for ministry leaders is how much our work is empowering others for success. For example, for about ten years part of my job was negotiating church planting funds from a national missions agency. Those funds would often flow to new churches many months after the negotiations had been completed. By the time the money arrived, my role would have been completely forgotten (if it was ever known!). The church planters who received the funds and the converts and churches that resulted often never knew about my role in the process.

A good way to purify your motives for leadership is to find ways to make others successful. When I saw those churches flourishing, I often left their services with a quiet satisfaction. I would pray, "Thank you, Lord, for letting me have a hand in their success. And, thanks for not letting anyone remember I had anything to do with it." Leaders can make decisions, launch processes, create systems, and empower people to be successful without any hint of their involvement. Like a show's producer, we can set the stage, employ the crew, choose the director, and handle all the logistics. But when the curtain goes up, we will not be anywhere on stage. Making others successful, and choosing to do it without expecting any recognition, is a surefire way to purify your leadership motives.

———◆———

Servant leadership is a worthy model. But do not be fooled into thinking servant leadership is about the job, the title, or the amount of the paycheck. Servant leadership is about the heart. It's primarily about motive. A servant leader is driven by his or her love for God and people.

Servant leadership is a character issue. As you achieve success in ministry—however you define it—the temptations to self-reliance or self-promotion grow greater. Leaving a leadership legacy requires resting your service on proper motives. When you're finished, you want people to remember the person you are more than the tasks you accomplished. Servant leaders leave a vapor trail of the sweet aroma of Jesus' humility formed in them.

CHAPTER SEVEN

Gaining Wisdom

WHEN I EVALUATE up-and-coming young executives, whether or not they have wisdom is a priority. It's not possible to learn wisdom. They either have wisdom or they don't." Those statements got my attention. The president of a major corporation and respected Christian businessman made them while we worked together on a leadership consortium. Our assignment was to define the core qualities for Christian leaders (which also got me thinking about writing this book).

While I respected the speaker, his statements about wisdom did not sound right to me. Those statements motivated an extended study of the subject of wisdom in the Bible. Insights from that study are the foundation of this chapter. Selected Scripture passages that support various sections of this chapter are included. Before I completed this study, about the only thing I knew the Bible taught about wisdom was that we are supposed to pray for it. Also, the only thing I did to try to increase my wisdom was pray about it. The Bible has much more to say about this important character quality for leaders.

My friend was right in his conviction about the importance of wisdom. Wisdom is an indispensable character quality for business executives. It is also essential for ministry leaders—in fact, for leaders in every field. But wisdom is not a mysterious quality some leaders have and others do not. Wisdom can be taught, learned, observed in the lives of leaders and measured by definable behaviors.

This means you can gain wisdom. You can become wiser and continue to grow in wisdom over a lifetime. Wisdom is not reserved for certain people or groups of people. Seeking wisdom is sometimes portrayed as trekking to visit an aged guru on a distant mountain. Other times it is assumed to be the sole purview of senior, seasoned leaders. These images do not reflect what the Bible teaches about wisdom. It is much more accessible. You can begin developing it now, no matter your situation or age.

The Development of Wisdom

You Can Learn to Be Wise

The Bible clearly indicates that wisdom is attainable. Furthermore, we are responsible to gain it.

A book of the Bible was written to reveal wisdom and how to get it. The first major purpose listed for the book of Proverbs is "gaining wisdom" (Prov. 1:2). Does it make sense that a book of the Bible would have the purpose of "gaining wisdom" if that were an impossible goal? Of course not.

A second encouragement is the way Proverbs portrays wisdom. On several occasions (see Prov. 8, for example), wisdom is personified as a woman calling out in the streets. Wisdom is calling for our attention, walking and waiting at the city gates, inviting us to a feast, and communicating her availability in other ways as well. Wisdom is certainly not hiding. On the contrary, it is personified as a woman aggressively trying to get our attention.

Proverbs and also Psalms have repeated admonitions for us to "get wisdom." Would God tell us to get something that is unavailable or unattainable? Again, no. God is not capricious. He instructs and enables us to achieve realistic goals.

But the best example of growing in wisdom is Jesus. As a young man, he "grew in wisdom" (Luke 2:52 NIV). Jesus is our model for life and leadership. He grew in wisdom; therefore, we can too. But where do you go to learn wisdom? What can you do to grow in wisdom?

First answer—God! God is described in the Bible as the only wise God, the ultimate source of wisdom (Rom. 16:27). God reveals himself and his wisdom through his Word (Ps. 19:7) and his works (Ps. 104:24). God's Word, the Bible, is the primary sourcebook for wisdom. Real wisdom comes from taking the Bible seriously, learning to apply it appropriately to complex life situations, and discerning its principles for today's realities.

God's creation and his subsequent works throughout history also reveal his wisdom. Part of learning wisdom from God's creation is observing nature. Particularly *ants* are singled out in Proverbs as examples of wise behavior! While this is much more subjective than learning from Scripture, it is interesting that the Bible speaks so often of God's works revealing his wisdom (Prov. 6:6; Ps. 104:24).

Second answer—people. Some people are farther down the wisdom road than others. Throughout the Bible we are instructed to observe the wise, seek counsel, and learn from the wise (Prov. 13:20; 19:20). Parents are particularly cited as a special source of wisdom for children of all ages (Prov. 4:11; 5:1; 29:15). What a pleasure to have the powerful generational blessing of wise parents to talk with about life!

Some of the wisest people are not necessarily the best educated. They are students of the Bible, of life, and of the ways God works with people and circumstances. They have an innate, reflective ability to discern how God is at work in a given situation and what principle or principles from his Word are pertinent. Making and keeping these friends must be a priority so you can learn from them.

So, in short, you can learn wisdom. You can grow in wisdom. Your best sources for wisdom are God's Word and works. Learn from his Word. Observe his works and learn from them. Another good source is wise people. Seek wise counselors—friends, parents, and mentors—and learn from them. All of these sources are precious assets for every leader to cultivate to develop wisdom.

Wisdom Is Revealed by Your Actions

One mistake about wisdom is thinking of it only as some ethereal ability to make good decisions or have sound judgment—like Solomon dividing the baby. Wisdom *is* the ability to make good decisions and have sound judgment, but it is more than that. In the Bible, wisdom is displayed by appropriate behavior.

For example, wise people exhibit at least fifteen behaviors listed in the Bible, most in Proverbs. All of these are observable actions. All of them demonstrate wisdom. In other words, you show your wisdom by what you do, by how you act, and by the choices you make.

The Bible says a wise person fears God (Prov. 3:7), speaks carefully (Prov. 10:19), is a lifelong learner (Prov. 10:14), is prudent (Prov. 14:8), gains new knowledge (Prov. 18:15), has discretion (Prov. 8:13), is open to correction (Prov. 9:8–9), demonstrates discernment (Prov. 10:13), wins people to faith in Jesus (Prov. 11:30), builds his or her family (Prov. 14:1), controls anger (Prov. 29:11), gives honor (Prov. 3:35), is morally pure (Prov. 7:4–5), relates well to parents (Prov. 10:1), and uses time appropriately (Eph. 5:15). These Scripture passages are representative of many that list these qualities.

All of these behaviors are easily observed. When you see a person doing these things, they are wise by the Bible's definition. When you see someone falling short in one of these areas, it indicates he or she needs to grow in wisdom. If you want to increase in wisdom, change your thinking on these important issues and behave differently. Wisdom is grounded in right thinking that produces right actions.

The Bible is also specific when it describes people who lack wisdom. Three categories of behavior consistently define the unwise. Amazingly, even in a postmodern culture, these actions are still generally considered marks of immaturity and bad choices.

Compulsive behavior or addictions (Prov. 20:1). Drunkenness is condemned throughout Scripture. Alcoholic beverages, particularly wine, were available in the biblical world and used by biblical characters. While the prevalence of their use and the potency of the beverages can be debated, abuse of alcohol was enough of a problem that it was repeatedly condemned in both the Old and New Testaments. The abuse of alcohol is always called unwise in the Bible.

Other potentially addictive behaviors, such as drug abuse and pornography, are not specifically mentioned in the context with drunkenness. While these temptations were available in biblical culture, they were not as prevalent as today. It is appropriate, however, to understand the prohibition on drunkenness in a broader sense. Drunkenness was specifically condemned, and by inference, all addictive behavior could be included. All indulgence leading to possible addiction is unwise.

Parents know the struggle of helping teenagers understand this. The biblical case for absolute abstinence from alcohol or other addictive behavior can be made, but not without some discussion and interpretation of Scripture. Any honest inquirer admits that. But the case for abstinence is easy to adopt when your goal is living wisely, as circumspectly as possible, without any hint of potentially destructive or compromising behavior. On that point, the Bible is crystal clear.

Teenagers, in their immaturity, often challenge this point and others like it. Their frequent question is "How much can I do and still not sin?" They want to live near the edge but not fall into sin. They do not yet understand that wisdom is not license to live on the edge of what might be allowable. Wisdom is making the choice to live far from the edge of what is permissible. Wisdom avoids all potentially addictive behavior.

Leaders understand this principle and are not deceived by their supposed strength. Many leaders have strong appetites. They like to eat heartily, drink merrily, and are convinced they are the exception to the consequences. Sometimes this arrogance leads to tampering with alcohol, drugs, pornography, or other potentially addictive behavior. Leaders convince themselves "they can handle it." They cannot.

When you involve yourself in any potentially addictive behavior, you are not wise! Your arrogance is fooling you. While there are sometimes immediate negative repercussions, God's warnings about certain behaviors are about the long-term consequences instead of the immediate results. Sure, one drink, one drug, or one evening on an Internet porn site may not destroy you. But how can you be sure your dabbling with destructive behavior will not lead to addictive catastrophe? You can't. Wisdom avoids dabbling with potentially destructive behavior. Wisdom pushes you away from the edge, not toward it.

Financial irresponsibility (Prov. 21:20). Growth in financial stewardship measures wisdom. The use of money, financial stewardship, and total financial responsibility are barometers of wisdom. Wise people recognize God as their monetary source, give generously to his work, manage the remainder of his provision carefully, live on their income, invest for the future, and put no trust in wealth.

Leaders often make good salaries and are expected to model sound personal financial management. They are also entrusted with significant financial decisions, sometimes involving large sums of money on behalf of their organizations. Financial irresponsibility, personal or corporate, reveals a lack of wisdom. This is not difficult to discern. Some simple questions can help analyze how a leader handles personal finances, which often predicts how he or she will manage corporate resources.

When interviewing a person for a leadership role, ask about their patterns of stewardship. Does the person live on his income? Does she pay her bills on time? Does he tithe and give offerings? Does she invest for the future and have an appropriate attitude toward wealth? If the answer is yes, chances are very good the person will also manage the organization's money well.

There are several red flags that reveal a problem with financial responsibility. One is living above your means. For example, your credit cards are maxed out. You live paycheck to paycheck. You obligate yourself for more than you can reasonably pay. You keep financial secrets from your spouse.

You ignore financial advice because you are sure you are the exception to the financial rules. These choices indicate personal financial irresponsibility.

How a leader handles his or her personal finances is an important barometer. It reveals wisdom, particularly related to personal finances. But it also reveals how the leader will manage an organization's finances and its overall submission to God's standards. In the long run, and particularly during times of financial duress, personal financial convictions will influence a leader's decisions for his organization. Observing sound personal financial practices is a good predictor of a leader's corporate responsibility, especially when the pressure mounts.

Another red flag is when a leader is not a generous giver. Ministry leaders often ask others to give generously and sacrificially to various projects. Sometimes these same leaders do not tithe, much less give additional offerings. One person said, "God told me, since I give my time, I don't have need to give my money." Wrong! Every ministry leader must model generosity. Every ministry leader must be a disciplined giver, exceeding the tithe, and setting the pace for those he leads.

Spending habits and giving decisions reveal a leader's core financial values. These financial practices measure and reveal wisdom. How you handle your money is a clear biblical indicator of your level of wisdom and your willingness to submit to God's standards in this very practical, tangible area of life.

Resenting correction (Prov. 15:12). Wise leaders invite correction and respond positively to it. They are lifelong learners, eager to improve themselves. They have an ease about them that is attractive to others. They are not know-it-alls or braggarts. They do not have delusions of adequacy. A leader growing in wisdom is approachable and interested in the opinions, perspectives, and insights of others.

This is an interesting contrast. The wiser you are, the more you will not think yourself wise. The more wisdom you gain, the more wisdom you will seek. Occasionally, students come to seminary with a misplaced goal. They come not to learn but to impress us with how much they already know. That is the opposite attitude of wisdom. Wise leaders are eager students, willing to learn, be taught, and gain new knowledge.

One negative expression of resisting correction is resistance to supervision or evaluation. God has given every leader a supervisor, usually a board or other group to whom he is accountable. Some leaders resent this relationship and resist supervision. They do not like regular performance reviews and discussion of their shortcomings. Hearing about areas of needed improvement is unwelcome.

Suggestions for continuing education or training are unheeded. Beware of these leaders! Their arrogance will be their downfall.

When I was interviewed to be a seminary president, one of the very perceptive questions was, "What is the annual review process in your current position and how do you respond to it?" Another good question was, "What are the weaknesses your past reviews have revealed and what are you doing about them?" Answering these questions revealed much about my openness to correction and willingness to learn in my new position. When you ask a similar question in an interview, the attitude of the responder is as important as the answers themselves. Wise leaders understand their need for supervision. They welcome honest dialogue about their work and seek ways to improve their performance. Unwise leaders resist and resent correction.

Wise leaders are also lifelong learners. They read books, watch videos, go to seminars and conferences, discuss new ideas with friends or mentors, and take advantage of other opportunities to learn and grow. Wise leaders learn new things. They are open to changing their mind, even about important subjects. One mentor challenged me when I was younger (and much more legalistic) to "stay alive all my life." He was concerned that my mind was already fossilizing! Wise leaders do not let that happen.

False Wisdom Can Fool You

Another interesting contrast in the Bible is between true and false wisdom. All good things, all godly things, have been counterfeited by the devil. Wisdom is no exception. True wisdom has clear origins; so does false wisdom. True wisdom has measurable results, as does false wisdom. True wisdom is readily available, but so is false wisdom. Leaders must be alert to the differences and seek the right kind of wisdom.

True wisdom is closely related to the gospel, to preaching about salvation. It is a manifestation of the Holy Spirit and found in relationship with Jesus Christ. You should pray for it (Paul did) and expect God to give it to you by his grace. True wisdom is revealed through humble living that demonstrates character shaped through your relationship with Jesus. We should strive to get it, while at the same time trusting God for it (1 Cor. 2:1–7; 12:8; Col. 1:28; 2:3; 4:5; 2 Tim. 3:15; Eph. 1:8, 17; 3:10; James 3:13–17).

False wisdom is not related to the gospel. Instead it points to idolatry and immorality. It attempts to confound the message of the cross but is instead confounded by the cross. False wisdom can masquerade as legalism, binding you with rules and regulations rather than freeing you by the Spirit. It can also throw off moral restraint, encouraging rejection of God's standards. False wisdom originates with the devil and produces all kinds of destructive behavior like envy, selfishness, immorality, and disorder (Rom. 1:22; 1 Cor. 1:18–27; 3:18–20; Col. 2:23; James 3:15–16).

Beware of leaders who have all the answers or who always have the final answer! Legalism produces leaders who claim all wisdom. They know how every Christian should dress, be entertained, raise their family, decide complex moral problems, and participate in church. False wisdom is so sure of itself. Leaders with false wisdom may seem humble, but they are really arrogant. They claim the final word on everything, but no matter how piously they pronounce it, it's still legalism.

Leaders with false wisdom, particularly leaders in public or political life, often make decisions contradicting the gospel and biblical standards. Some of these are suave, sophisticated leaders. They want to sound insightful and wise, claiming to build on ethical foundations to take our society to new levels of awareness. For example, many leaders who are attempting to redefine marriage fit this category. They are sharply dressed, carefully coiffed, media-ready spokespersons with well-reasoned, high-sounding arguments. They claim a high goal—equal rights for all. They seem to be advocating a liberating position. But in reality, they are in dogmatic denial of God's standards. We are not ascending when we follow these leaders. We are spiraling downward.

Some leaders cloak false wisdom in popular or right-sounding positions. Again, marriage revisionists are a good example. They have positioned gay marriage as a struggle similar to the civil rights movement. Thankfully, many African-American leaders have called their hand on this charade. Cloaking false wisdom (gay rights) in the cloak of true wisdom (civil rights) may be a slick strategy, but it's still wrong.

Religious leaders sometimes fall into this trap. American Christian television is often an embarrassment to biblical Christianity. Designer clothes, make-up artists, and elaborate set designs make the preachers and presenters so adorable. What they are saying *must* be right. Wrong! When religious leaders promote greed and envy by a get-rich-quick gospel, they are just as guilty of demonstrating false wisdom as any misguided politician.

No matter how smooth the operator or how ear-tickling the information, false wisdom is always destructive. Real leaders, wise leaders, work hard to avoid these traps and teach their followers to do the same. Be on your guard!

Becoming Wiser

Gaining wisdom does not happen overnight. Becoming wiser is not a one-two-three, step-by-step process. There is no simplistic formula that rushes the results. Gaining wisdom is a process—a slow, continuing process that unfolds over a lifetime. Since one of the characteristics of a wise person is lifelong learning, you need to settle in for the long haul. Having accepted that, there are some specific, practical things you can do to speed up this process. Doing them again and again, over a lifetime, will help you become wiser.

Seek God as your Source of wisdom. Wisdom comes from God. Make a conscious decision to reject worldly wisdom and seek God's wisdom. Raise your spiritual antennae and ask for more discernment about false wisdom that may have crept into your thinking. Intentionally adopt a Christian worldview and seek to apply biblical principles to every area of life. Develop a healthy fear of God, which is the beginning of wisdom. The fear of God is discussed in greater detail in chapter nine.

Draw on spiritual resources for wisdom. Since wisdom is found in a relationship with God, be sure of your salvation! You will not discover true wisdom apart from humbling yourself, coming to God through Jesus, and determining to learn submissively from him.

Most Christian leaders, hopefully, have made that foundational decision. Next, read and study the Bible to learn God's Word and discover how he works. A leader must read the Bible regularly, with a goal of daily. This is devotional Bible reading, not sermon or Bible study preparation. Many leaders leave off this basic discipline that builds wise thinking over a lifetime.

Regular Bible reading is God's opportunity to shape your life incrementally. When Michelangelo painted the Sistine Chapel, he was on scaffolding within arm's reach of the ceiling. Each day he painted only a small portion. Yet, in his mind, he could see the entire ceiling as it would ultimately appear. God is like that with you. Each day he paints a little understanding into your life through his Word. You only see the little bit you learn that day, but God sees the big picture. Ultimately, the daily shaping by God's Word creates a dramatic impact. Your entire life takes new form and wise thinking becomes the norm.

In addition to Bible reading, in-depth Bible study is also required to learn wisdom. Serious Bible study—word by word, book by book, topic by topic—is part of how a leader learns wisdom. That's why many Christian leaders profit from college and seminary training. Some ministers, however, occasionally complain, "There are so many ministry situations seminary did not teach me to handle." My answer is always, "You're exactly right, we didn't." This admission often surprises a critic. But it's true. Our seminary does not teach every skill needed for every ministry situation. But we do teach principles of effective ministry and tools for a lifetime of serious Bible study. If you are using "they never taught me in seminary" as a cop-out, stop it! Get busy studying your Bible and discover fresh wisdom for your ministry from God and his Word.

Finally, pray for wisdom. That's all I knew about getting wisdom when I started this study. Prayer is still a primary source of wisdom. There is something special and powerful about getting on your knees and asking God for wisdom, knowing he has promised to give it. After praying for wisdom, you will be amazed how God works through you to make difficult decisions. Generally, however, prayer for wisdom seems to work best when used in conjunction with the other strategies in this chapter.

Learn from wise people. God can teach you wisdom through others who are more mature than you are. Parents have already been mentioned as a source of wisdom. If you are blessed with wise parents, draw on their wisdom often. Some develop relationships with surrogate parents, drawing on their wisdom as well.

There are also other ways to learn from wise people. For example, you can study wise biblical characters—particularly Jesus and Solomon. One way to experience Solomon's wisdom is reading the chapter of Proverbs that corresponds to the date of the month. My oldest son joined me in this practice when he was a teenager. As a young adult, he is becoming a confidant and trusted advisor largely because of how his thinking has been shaped by Solomon. You should also include heavy doses of the Gospels in your Bible reading plan. Hearing from Jesus, the wisest man who ever lived, as often as possible will also increase your wisdom. Observing Jesus deal with people is also a vital example of wisdom in relationships. Learning how Jesus handled people and situations effectively will enable you to do the same.

You can also learn wisdom from historical figures by reading biographies. Christian biographies are very helpful, but biographies of secular leaders can also help you gain wisdom. Read life stories of American presidents, world leaders, famous explorers, sports heroes, and military generals for broad examples of how leaders perform in challenging situations. Biographies like these can help you in two ways. First, you will see true wisdom demonstrated and learn how to respond in different situations. Second, you will also see false wisdom and how to avoid bad decisions and tragic mistakes. Both good and bad examples, good and bad outcomes are instructive as you discern how leaders attempt to live wisely.

You can also learn wisdom from people you know and from public figures you admire. Several wise friends have counseled, mentored, sponsored, or otherwise shaped me over the years. Some of these are peers and some are older men who have taken an interest in me. Well-known Christian leaders you admire can teach you wisdom, even from a distance. Sometimes, we can observe wise leaders from a distance and see how they handle controversy, manage circumstances, and stay above the fray of petty controversy. From their examples, we increase our wisdom to handle problems we are facing.

Benchmarks for Your Progress

Since gaining wisdom is a lifelong process, is it possible to measure your progress? Yes! There are several benchmarks you can use to measure growth in wisdom.

Benchmark 1: You are growing in your ability to see life's situations from God's perspective. As you grow in wisdom, you will more and more naturally view situations as God sees them. You will spontaneously start flipping through the note cards in your mind for applicable biblical principles when you confront a problem. You will find yourself thinking, *There's a proverb that relates to this problem* or *I remember how King David resolved this problem* or *In a biography, a missionary worked through this same dilemma* or *One of my mentors faced a similar incident.* As thinking about life from

God's perspective becomes more and more natural, you will know you are growing in wisdom.

Benchmark 2: You are able to relate biblical *principles* to challenging life situations (rather than depending on legalistic proof-texting). Some contemporary problems are not mentioned specifically in the Bible. The leader must know God and his Word well enough to recognize the applicable principles for solving thorny problems. As you grow in this area, you will discover that the Bible speaks to every issue and human dilemma. It may not speak chapter and verse, but it can speak principle upon precept. Wise leaders are growing in their capacity to use God's Word this way.

Benchmark 3: You choose best behavior over license in questionable situations. As a young Christian, I wanted to live on the edge of acceptability to God. My question was, "How far can I go (morally, sexually, financially) and still not be technically disobedient to God?" As I have grown in wisdom, my new question is "Father, what behavior best models your grace?" Wisdom does not look for loopholes; it strives for holiness without legalistic overtones. Wisdom lives on a margin, not on the edge courting disaster. Wisdom pushes away from the edge instead of straining to peer over it.

Benchmark 4: You have a growing humility about your decisions, positions, perspectives, and insights. Wisdom doesn't blow its own horn! Wise leaders have a growing confidence in their insight but also have a corresponding humility. One of my wisest friends is also very slow to give his opinion. He often sits quietly while others with far less insight speak. Wise leaders are often like that. They know what they know and are more than willing to share when asked. But they do not parade their wisdom. Wise leaders are also very patient with people who disagree with them. They do not have to be agreed with because, deep down, they know they are right and are willing to wait for it to become evident.

———◆———

So there is more to getting wisdom than just praying for it. Wisdom can be learned. Wisdom is a required character quality for leaders in every field. So, get busy learning wisdom. Measure yourself by these benchmarks and continually evaluate your progress as you grow in wisdom. Someday, your leadership legacy will include wise decisions and wise behavior. Effective leaders do not settle for less!

CHAPTER EIGHT

Practicing Discipline

Children believe becoming an adult means they can do whatever they want, whenever they want. If only it were so! No wonder my oldest son, when he turned twenty-one, told his younger siblings, "Stay a kid as long as you can!" Adulthood equals responsibility. Being an adult means you fulfill your responsibilities without supervision. Leadership requires you do this to an even greater degree than your followers. Leadership calls for fulfilling self-supervised responsibilities, often duties only you know you have.

Leadership requires discipline. Discipline is the ability to regulate your behavior by principle rather than impulse, reason rather than emotion, and long-range results rather than immediate gratification. Discipline is doing what is best, not what is easiest. You are disciplined when you choose to do difficult things and make them a habit.

Ministry leaders must develop greater levels of self-control than their followers for several reasons.

First, leaders are expected to model proper behavior in many different areas. Ministry leaders set the pace in everything from parenting skills to personal witnessing to financial management. While no leader is a perfect model in any area, every leader is expected to be an acceptable model in multiple areas.

Second, a leader's behavior is limited in ways followers' behavior is not. Leaders are required to be circumspect in their choices. Some actions might be acceptable to others, but leaders avoid even a hint of impropriety. Clothing choices are a good example. Christian leaders dress with deference to the age, cultural, and societal expectations they encounter. Leaders are not obligated to dress a certain way, but wise leaders know their clothing choices are significant. Self-control is required to accept and make these lifestyle choices in the best interest of their ministry purpose.

Another reason leaders must be self-disciplined is their workload. Everyone is busy! But schedule demands for leaders are often very challenging. Once commitments are made, they are hard to adjust without disappointing others by mangling their plans. Discipline is required to control what gets on the schedule and then make sure what is scheduled actually gets done.

Some leaders believe their role is to work less and keep others busy. This is a recipe for short tenure among your followers. Good leaders manage their schedule and are considerate of employees or volunteers. A healthy experience for a leader is to be a follower in a different setting or for a season. Pastors who have moved to "member only" roles in churches often change their perspective on ministry involvement. They realize how difficult it is to manage personal demands and meet the expectations of church membership.

Finally, leaders must be self-controlled because they do not usually have close supervision. Leaders, particularly ministry leaders, often have wide latitude in determining their schedules, activities, projects, and methods. Pastors are often largely on their own with little direct supervision. Freedom from external control requires a leader to be disciplined enough to do the right thing, while creating necessary structures to help him stay on track.

Fortunately, God has not left you alone to learn discipline, nor does he expect you to develop it on your own. He has given you a powerful Ally, a Source and Resource for developing discipline. He has given you the indwelling Holy Spirit.

Discipline Is a Spiritual Issue

A puzzling passage in the Bible is Galatians 5:22–23, which lists the fruit of the Spirit. The fruit are the results of allowing the Holy Spirit to influence, dominate, or control our lives. The last fruit of the Spirit is *self*-control. The *self* part is the puzzling part. If self-control, or self-discipline, is a Spirit-produced result, what part does the *self* play? Doesn't self-control and Spirit-fruit seem like a contradiction?

The answer is no. The fact that self-control or self-discipline is Spirit produced only underscores the need to depend on the Spirit for developing this important quality. No fleshly effort will please God or build true discipline. Self-discipline refers to *self* as the object of discipline rather than its source. Even though discipline is learned, and self is the object of the discipline, the motivation and power to develop discipline comes from the Spirit.

Biblical writers use different illustrations to teach about discipline. For example, farmers, soldiers, and athletes are all favorite analogies (2 Tim. 2:3–7). Paul used runners and boxers to illustrate his need for discipline (1 Cor. 9:24–27). He used the illustration of the boxer to describe himself, writing, "I do not . . . box like one who beats the air. Instead, I discipline [beat] my body and bring it under strict control."

Christian leadership requires discipline, self-control, and the ability to do the right thing in the face of unusual circumstances. One of the most disciplined leaders in the Bible was Joseph, Jesus' stepfather. Joseph encountered a very unusual and challenging circumstance. Mary was pregnant! He demonstrated remarkable self-control by not ending his relationship with Mary. Joseph had every right to do so but chose to marry her instead. He reared Jesus in the face of what must have been intense critical scrutiny by the community. Joseph did this without any record of rancor, response, or retaliation to whatever he or his family may have faced.

But the more remarkable testimony to Joseph's self-control is he "married her [Mary] but did not know her intimately until she gave birth to a son" (Matt. 1:24–25). Mary and Joseph, a unique couple in many ways, were also very human. We can reasonably assume, under normal circumstances, they would have initiated their sexual relationship after marriage.

Joseph, however, maintained his sexual self-control and kept Mary a virgin until after the birth of Jesus. While God was responsible for the virgin *conception* of Jesus, Joseph was responsible for the virgin *birth*. What a trust Joseph was given! God called him to protect Mary's virginity so Jesus would be born of a virgin.

Clearly, discipline is a desirable quality for leaders. Desirable but not easily attained. Paul's image of self-pummeling is not pleasant but communicates how seriously a leader must develop discipline. Practicing a disciplined lifestyle will be painful. The pain must sometimes be self-inflicted. The Spirit will empower you to bring yourself under control. Here are some practical steps you can take to build more discipline into your life.

Master a Difficult Area

When we were first married, I was the wimpy "before" picture in the bodybuilding ads. Regular meals and hours filled in the skinny places. Soon my ribs no longer showed! My weight stabilized for several years. Then, one day, I woke up fat. Not obese, just chubby. I jiggled when I walked. I felt sluggish. I had the spare tire, love-handle look.

For the first time in my life, I had to change my eating habits. *No problem,* I thought. Big problem, it turned out! Eating had become a hobby. I enjoyed it. I discovered it was very difficult to control my appetite. At first, I tried choosing different foods. But my weight stayed about the same. My issue was not food choice but lack of self-control. The real problem was not my weight. It was deeper than that. I had to control the urge to eat. I needed a new level of self-discipline.

To break a long-standing habit like this required some dramatic action. My goal became breaking the control my appetite had over me. My strategy was several multi-day fasts over a one-year period. My objectives were to master my eating habits, break the tyranny of my appetite, and overcome the temptation of hunger pangs. When you fast for several days, you reach a point where you no longer feel hungry. It is an exhilarating and empowering experience! Reaching that point would be both difficult and liberating. Reaching it repeatedly over several months was essential to the process.

When the hunger pangs abated during the first fast, I had come to a new level of self-control. It had been a hard few days. I felt hungry, really hungry! My stomach thought someone had cut my throat and kept sending urgent "feed me" signals to my brain. My family, of course, kept eating, which provided a thrice-daily temptation. But I made it. Eventually, I no longer felt hungry. I was no longer tempted to eat. I had mastered my appetite, so I broke the first fast.

This fasting experience was not primarily about seeking spiritual insight. Most fasting has that purpose. This fast was about breaking my appetite. It was about getting control of my urges. It was about being master of my body. So, when the first fast accomplished its purpose I ended it. A few months later, I repeated this process. This time it was easier but still challenging. Again, however, I felt the same exhilarating release from the controlling influence of my appetite.

A few months later, I repeated the process the third time. This time, when the hunger pangs started, my response was easy. "Beg all you want," I told my appetite, "you're not in charge anymore." The third fast was not difficult at all. When it ended,

I knew I had control of my appetite. From then on, I knew I would be in charge of my eating habits.

These fasting experiences happened many years ago. Since then, I have maintained my weight within an appropriate range (although it is getting harder as I get older!). Occasionally, the old temptations or holiday feasting get me off track. But these diversions are easily corrected with a few days of careful eating. I do not diet (although I try to eat nutritiously), but I do control the amount I eat.

The point of this process, however, was not primarily about food, weight loss, appetite control, or spiritual insight. It was about mastering a difficult area, therefore increasing my self-control. In doing so, something remarkable happened. I discovered a new level of discipline in other areas as well. After this experience, I was more able to handle sexual temptation and control my anger—two other very challenging areas. Mastering a difficult area has a "spillover" effect in our lives.

So, choose a difficult area and master it. Create a year-long project to establish a greater level of discipline in one area of your life. For example, turn off the television for one year. Save a significant amount of money every month to break your spending habit. Choose an exercise—such as walking or cycling—and do it rain or shine. Get control of your anger by significantly changing how you react to troubling situations.

Choose a difficult area for *you*. Do not try to do more than one at a time. Choose one area and master it. You will be surprised at the freedom this will bring. You will also be delighted how much more disciplined you will be in other areas as a by-product of this effort.

Work on a Special Project

Practice does not make perfect. Practice makes permanent. Practicing discipline makes it a permanent life skill. While mastering a very difficult area can lead to lifelong breakthroughs of discipline, choosing an occasional special discipline project can practice and sharpen self-control.

For example, a group of coworkers formed a Scripture memory group. We worked for one year to improve our Scripture memory skills and requisite self-discipline. We met at the beginning of each month for thirty minutes to choose a passage and a partner from the group. Then, throughout the month, partners held each other accountable to learn the passage. Because most of us traveled, we would often leave voice mail messages of attempts to quote the passage. Since we changed partners every month, no one drifted or became complacent. We all stayed sharp holding each other accountable.

We worked on this project for a year. We memorized several passages from the Bible that improved our overall spiritual self-discipline. Once again, a concentrated effort to improve discipline in one area had a broader impact. Participants also reported more discipline in areas such as prayer and Bible reading.

Another year, another group of coworkers formed a witnessing accountability group. We met monthly to discuss our attempts at personal evangelism. We prayed for one another, for the people we were witnessing to, and for sensitivity to divine appointments. Once again, the accountability of the group produced results. Not only did we witness more consistently; our overall spiritual discipline was again heightened. Group members became more sensitive to the needs of people God brought across their paths.

These special projects do not always require a group effort. For example, you might develop a predetermined annual reading program. Each year, choose a subject, a group of books, a type of literature, or an author and lay out a reading plan. Staying focused on the plan not only deepens your knowledge in a specific field each year; it also reinforces discipline in others, such as time management. Making time to read instead of wasting time (such as while traveling), spills over and improves discipline in other areas as well.

The first key to both individual and group projects like these is setting realistic goals and expecting reasonable results. The second is not making the project so easy you avoid a real challenge. I did not learn all the Scripture verses, have a glowing witnessing report every month, or read every book I ever planned to read. My goals were reasonable, yet challenging. Being honest about the level of accomplishment is part of learning discipline and allowing the project to really change you.

Be realistic. Be transparent. In appropriate ways, be hard on yourself! Choose good projects with attainable goals. Do your best and be honest with your level of success. Work with a group for encouragement and motivation. The special discipline projects you create will shape you in a specific area. But the pleasant surprise is they will also impact you in many other areas as well.

Build Habits That Work for You

As a boy, my mom constantly corrected my three worst habits—biting my nails, resting elbows on the table, and talking too much. I have successfully overcome the first two! We all have bad habits. Most of our attention regarding habits focuses on correcting bad ones. But building good habits is also productive. Good habits can be as helpful as our bad habits are distracting.

A habit is a built-in pattern of behavior requiring little or no use of the will. It is ingrained behavior. Habits are actions you do automatically. They are your default mode. Habits, good and bad, are learned behavior. Most of them are learned subconsciously, as part of your upbringing, and influenced heavily by your early social interactions. You hitch your pants a certain way, sit in the same place at the table each night, or drum your fingers when you get nervous. These habits can change, but it usually takes an intentional choice to do it.

You probably assume your habits will change as you become a more disciplined person. That is exactly backward! The process works the other way. First, you make an intentional choice to change your habits. Then a more disciplined lifestyle ensues. Trying to change your life without first adjusting your habits will be frustrating. You will continually fall back into old patterns. You must start new habits and stop old ones. In this transaction, greater discipline is realized and lifestyle changes result.

During college years, getting up early for daily Bible reading and prayer was a challenge. Daily devotions were an up-and-down, hit-and-miss effort. Establishing this habit seemed impossible. As a young pastor, my devotional life continued to be a problem. My attempts to solve this problem always focused on being more committed to devotional practices, not addressing the real problem. The real problem was my bad habit of staying up too late.

Solving the devotional problem required new discipline in a seemingly unrelated area. Developing

the habit of going to bed at the same time and getting up at the same time as often as possible was the
key. Waking up early and feeling rested is no longer
much of a problem. Since I am more alert, having
more consistent devotions is easier. My devotional
discipline improved when I stopped focusing on
being more committed to my devotions and simply
established new sleep habits.

Changing a habit can also lead to a more disciplined lifestyle in other areas. One leader wanted
to spend more time with his young children. His
habit was morning coffee and the newspaper to
start the day, followed by an early trip to the office.
He made the choice to change his morning routine
to include helping his children get ready for school,
eating breakfast with them, and driving them to
school. He solved his problem by developing new
morning routine habits.

A pastor wanted more disciplined morning
study time. He was in the habit of arriving at about
the same time as the rest of his office staff, park-
ing in the same spot, entering through the main
entrance, and visiting with many people on the way
to his study. His social nature often turned this into
a lengthy distraction. He solved his problem by
establishing a new arrival routine. He arrived a few
minutes earlier than the rest of the staff, parked in
an alternative location, entered a side door, and went
straight to his office. By doing so, he eliminated the

distraction of the morning social hour and became much more disciplined in his study. And, when his messages for the week were finished, he could enjoy fellowship without the nagging sense that he was neglecting his preparation for preaching.

A church planter with young children at home and his office in his car was frustrated by his poor study habits. Working on his messages late at night and early in the morning while his children slept left him fatigued and moody. He solved his problem by establishing the habit of study at a nearby retreat center. One day each week was spent holed up working on his messages. No phone, no distractions, and no exceptions! Creating this weekly habit gave him the routine study time he needed.

A denominational leader moved from a distant state and often talked about how things had been done "back home." He really wanted to break the habit of constantly referring to his former place of leadership. He asked his coworkers to charge him a dollar every time he mentioned his home state. It did not take long for that habit to be broken! Doing so enabled him to be more disciplined in his focus on future challenges, not past ministry successes.

Changing habits to improve self-discipline requires transactional thinking. Many leaders want to change or add new behaviors without altering or stopping current patterns. That is not usually possible. Most of the time, old behavior has to stop before new patterns can be established. Plan a behavioral transaction when you consider starting a new habit. For every new habit you want to solidify, stop or significantly change the old behavior limiting the change.

Control Your Emotions

A significant challenge and responsibility for leaders is controlling their emotions. Leaders are expected to be cool under pressure. Developing self-control of emotions is vital because ministry leaders often find themselves in very intense situations. Self-discipline is required to maintain emotional and spiritual equilibrium during stressful circumstances.

Leaders must learn to control many emotions, but the two most prominent are grief and anger. Christian leaders are with people during times of profound loss and interpersonal tension. We are often present during death and bereavement, terminal illness, sick children, lost jobs, and teenage pregnancy. We are there when church members argue, difficult decisions are debated, employees are terminated, and volunteers are displaced. These are stressful, grief-inducing, anger-causing circumstances.

Often ministry leaders, because of love for the people involved, get caught up in the moment. Compassion calls for us to be honest with our feelings and demonstrate them appropriately. The key word is *appropriately.* Followers need leaders who can model appropriate grief and anger management in the midst of loss or conflict. They need leaders who minister rather than experience cathartic moments during crisis.

Managing grief. Sometimes, the ministry relationships are so personal your emotions will be quite difficult to manage. My friend Adam played baseball on several teams with my oldest son. His father and I coached together and our families became friends. We shared meals and good times at each other's homes. Our friendship was genuine and lasting. Little did we know our friendship would involve such deep pain.

Tragically, Adam was killed in the war in Iraq. It was as if our world stopped spinning. The cost of the war on terror became very personal—and very high. Adam's family asked me to officiate his memorial service along with a general and the governor of his state. The service was filled with poignant memories and emotions. We watched video greetings from fellow soldiers in Iraq, heard moving tributes from the military and civic leaders, and saw a beautiful presentation from Adam's family about his life.

The service included full military honors, including a rotating honor guard at attention beside the casket throughout the two-hour service. The burial procession was more than one hundred cars long. The walk to the grave was led by a full bagpipe corps and escorted by dozens of men in uniform from all branches of military and public service.

Keeping my emotions in check was difficult. But what the family and mourners needed from me was competent leadership through a grieving process, not a public display of my feelings. The focus had to be on their needs. My purpose was giving them permission in a safe atmosphere to grieve their incredible loss. Part of guiding that service was leading some people from denial into grief.

Another emotional situation involved childbirth. A young father, frantic because of birth complications his wife was experiencing, asked me to hurry to the hospital. When I had arrived, he rushed me into the delivery room shouting, "We're so glad you're here. My wife needs you!" The nurses were urgently scurrying to do their jobs. The doctor was intensely working to save both mother and child. A very frightened young woman grabbed my arm and shrieked, "Pray, please pray."

For the next few minutes, I held one hand and arm while her husband held the other. The nurses kept working. The doctor kept trying. The mother kept pushing. Finally, the baby emerged and was rushed to intensive care. The focus changed to stabilizing the mother. Fortunately, all had a happy ending. For years, on the child's birthday, the family sent me a photo and update about how his life had progressed.

During the crisis, my emotions were all over the map. For awhile, my grief almost overwhelmed me as I imagined helping a father deal with a dead child and seriously ill wife. Then I feared telling the couple their child might be seriously injured or handicapped. These were my friends!

While this was happening, these friends needed a leader. They were counting on me to control my grief, fear, and other emotions. My focus had to be on their needs. Leaders are expected to manage their emotions during a crisis and keep the needs of their followers the priority. Self-control enables you to manage emotions like grief. Self-discipline does not deny your emotions or your emotional needs. It simply gives you the spiritual power to keep your focus on meeting the needs of your followers.

Self-control does not mean you deny your grief or model fake stoicism. Controlling grief means you express it appropriately. Debrief with your spouse, a staff member, church leader, or trusted friend. Talk through your grief with those in the grief-inducing situation. Shed tears with the hurting in the right setting. These are appropriate ways to manage your grief without slipping into denial. Leaders implement solid strategies to manage grief. These enable you to keep the focus on your followers and handle your emotions effectively during trying times.

Managing anger. Perhaps the most important emotion for a leader to manage is anger. Leaders get angry. Sometimes, leaders get very angry and lash out at followers, associates, and fellow believers. Because leaders have greater influence, their anger has the potential for greater damage.

It took me a long time to learn this principle. One of my earliest memories in ministry is an angry outburst I unleashed on a young woman. My reason? I thought she made an unwise decision that embarrassed me. Looking back, the intensity of my legalism and mean-spirited attack astound me. When I finished my tirade, she was in tears. I remember feeling self-satisfied and thinking, *I really straightened her out.* All I really did was devastate her.

Another time I made some cutting remarks to a person who worked for me. His performance was substandard and reflected poorly on me (or so I thought). So I unloaded on him. Rather than correct his performance, all I did was deflate his spirit and damage his loyalty to me.

Slamming doors also works well to let people know how you really feel about what they have done or not done. Nothing speaks louder, right? I am embarrassed that I once thought this was a good way to motivate someone. Yelling at my children when they frustrated me, snapping at my wife, or lecturing players I coached were all futile demonstrations of anger. All of this became clear to me one night on a baseball field.

A fine young man was working with me as an assistant coach. He really looked up to me. As a young husband holding down a full-time job and going to college, he was sacrificing to help with the team. He made a split-second decision while coaching third base that made me angry. I let him know, in very plain terms, how I felt and how inadequate he was. The look in his eyes still haunts me.

My friend was devastated. He admired me and wanted to please me. He probably had me on too high a pedestal but, nonetheless, I was up there! As my ire spilled out on him, his shoulders slumped. Color drained from his face. His eyes, usually vibrant, lost luster and became like limp pools. Even though I apologized later that night, the damage was done. It took months to recover our relationship.

That night, something happened in me. I realized, as a leader, how much people are influenced by my opinion of them—for good or bad. My opinion matters more than a peer's opinion. What I communicate can control how a person feels about himself. When I am angry with people, they take it personally. My responsibility to manage my anger became very clear.

Managing anger, like managing grief, does not mean denying it. It means you learn to express your anger appropriately (Eph. 4:26–27). Jesus modeled this. He was occasionally angry and expressed it

(Mark 3:5; Matt. 21:12–13). Managing anger means you have the self-discipline, like Jesus, to express it appropriately. Controlling your anger and how you express it are essential for effective leadership. You can learn to manage your anger and express it appropriately by using these simple steps.

First, understand that anger is a result of feeling threatened. When you are threatened, you feel angry. It really is that simple. Lower your threat level by understanding your security in Jesus Christ. The more you practice the securing presence of Jesus, the fewer issues will anger you.

Second, label anger for what it really is. Call it anger. Don't say you are frustrated, put out, put off, or upset. End the denial. Admit to yourself and others, "I'm angry." Labeling anger is a key step to managing it appropriately.

Third, talk about why you are angry. Learn to talk about your anger, not talk while you are angry. Rather than lashing out in anger, learn to say, "I'm angry with you and I want to talk about it" or "I'm angry right now. I'd like to come back and talk about this later." Talk about your anger rather than acting it out. Yelling, slamming doors, peeling your tires, making obscene gestures, throwing things, or striking another person are never positive expressions of anger for a leader.

Fourth, manage circumstances that make you more vulnerable to anger. Most people become angry more easily when tired, hungry, or stressed. Understand these situations and manage them more effectively. Be alert to predictable circumstances that make you and your followers more susceptible to becoming angry.

Finally, accept the biblical conclusion that anger does not accomplish God's purposes (James 1:20). If you are using your anger to manipulate, intimidate, or otherwise control people, you are misusing anger. You may get short-term results, but you will demoralize your followers. While they may not confront you, they will simply drift away. Leaders who vent their anger through harsh preaching or speaking may build the crowd for awhile. But eventually, people drift away from consistent verbal abuse—even so-called "prophetic" preaching.

———◆———

Leadership requires self-discipline. Leaders must be self-controlled. While the Holy Spirit enables you to develop discipline, you are still responsible to do it. You will continually battle the temptation to self-justification for self-satisfying or self-promoting behavior. As a leader, though, you are called to a higher standard—self-discipline, self-control. Get ready for the lifelong challenge of living the disciplined life of a ministry leader.

CHAPTER NINE

Showing Courage

PEOPLE ARE AFRAID of everything from spiders and snakes to speaking in public. Most leaders get over their fear of public speaking but still struggle with many other fears. Leaders fear public ridicule, disappointing their followers or families, losing their positions of influence (and their paycheck), or embarrassing themselves with a bad decision or public gaffe.

Some leaders bluster and posture, claiming to be without fear. Nice act! Leaders are human, not superhuman, which means we all struggle with fear. A better strategy than denial is needed to handle fear. Understanding fear, how to confront it, and how to be courageous will serve you better than mastering the self-deception of denial.

Figuring Out Fear

Take heart! If you struggle with fear you are in good company. Fear is a very common problem in the Bible. There are more than 600 references in the Bible related to fear. The list of biblical characters who felt fear reads like a spiritual hall of fame: Adam, Abraham, Sarah, Lot, Isaac, Jacob, Rachel, Moses, Rahab, Joshua, Ruth, Samuel, David, Mephibosheth, Saul, Hezekiah, Elijah, Solomon, Jehosophat, Ahaz, Daniel, Joseph, Peter, Paul, and John.

All of these leaders were afraid of something. Several biblical leaders were told "do not be afraid," implying they also felt fear. Check out this list: Adam, Abraham, Hagar, Isaac, Jacob, Moses, Joshua (four times!), Isaiah, David, Joseph, Daniel, Zechariah, Mary, Jairus, Peter, Paul, John, the shepherds, and the women at the tomb. Again, this is good company.

Poor Joshua! God told him repeatedly not to be afraid. We normally think of Joshua as a warrior leading Israel into the Promised Land. He did lead them boldly, all while struggling with his fears. Leaders are not exempt from fearful feelings, but they are required to overcome them and lead.

Fear is also an old problem. There is no mention of fear as part of God's creation. However, the first emotion mentioned in the Bible *after* sin entered the world was fear (Gen. 3:10). This does not mean that fear is always a sin. After all, we are repeatedly told in the Bible to "fear the Lord." Sin entered the world and marred the concept of fear. No longer would fearing the Lord be the only expression of fear. Now, like everything else good and godly, fear was warped. Fearing the Lord (good fear) was lost and fearing everything else (bad fear) emerged.

Bad fear has predictable results, again emerging from the first story of people whose fears controlled them. Adam and Eve were afraid so they hid from God. At least one indication you have bad fear is that it controls you. This expresses itself in two ways.

First, fear is sinful when it makes you do something you know is wrong or you do not want to do. People such as Elijah (1 Kings 19:3), Peter (Mark 9:6), Sarah (Gen. 18:15), and Isaac (Gen. 26:7) all had this experience. Fear can cause you to go along with questionable decisions or allow others to control you. You are disgusted with yourself but cannot seem to hold your ground. When that happens, fear has control.

Second, fear is sinful when it keeps you from doing what you know you should do. Leaders sometimes do not speak up against injustice, hold employees accountable, or confront unruly church members because they are afraid. They know what they need to do but just cannot do it. Once again, destructive fear takes control. Joseph of Arimathea (John 19:38) had this problem. His fear of the Jews kept him from identifying himself as a follower of Jesus.

Your positive leadership legacy will be undermined if fear controls you. Bad fear always leaves
a destructive legacy. Part of this legacy is missing
God's best. Remember the story of the twelve spies
who spied out the land God was giving Israel? Ten
spies gave a bad report, prompted by fear of the
"giants in the land," and missed the blessings God
had for them. Fear kept the spies, and ultimately
their followers, from experiencing God's best. You
miss God's best when fear controls you. Sadly, you
also shortchange your followers.

Bad fear also keeps you from using the gifts
God has given you. In the parable of the talents
(Matt. 25:14–28), fear caused one servant to bury
what the master had given him. The servants who
used their talents got more talents. The one who
buried his talent lost his opportunity for future service. Fear can keep you from using your gifts and
experiencing even greater opportunity for service.

Fear can also have devastating consequences
when it keeps you from making good decisions.
Lot lived in Sodom with his wife and two daughters. Two angels, disguised as men, came to Lot's
home to warn him of impending destruction. He
was told to flee to the mountains for safety. But Lot
appealed to be allowed to live in Zoar since he perceived the journey too arduous.

When fire fell and destroyed Sodom and
Gomorrah, Lot changed his mind. He "was afraid to

live in Zoar" (Gen. 19:30), so he took his two daughters and hid in a cave. Time passed. The daughters
became alarmed that their father would die without an heir. They got Lot drunk and had incestuous
relations with him. Both women became pregnant.
The results: one birthed the father of the Moabites,
the other the father of the Ammonites. Lot acted
in fear. He fathered rank enemies of Israel, which
has been tormented for generations. Fear kept Lot
from making a good decision and opened the door
for a series of horrible consequences.

The fears that keep most leaders from making
good decisions involve relationships. You fear hurting people, hurting relationships with or among
people, or the painful consequences of making
personal or personnel decisions. Because churches
and ministry organizations are "people intensive,"
these kinds of fears predominate.

A good example is the decision to change a
person's job assignment or terminate him. This is a
gut-wrenching decision for many Christian leaders.
We fear hurting the person and the possible negative results among coworkers. Fear keeps us from
making timely decisions in this area, often to the
detriment of the employee and our organization.
Another example is being afraid to speak up on a
controversial matter or confront persons who may
disagree with you (and cause conflict if you oppose
them or their ideas).

These fears immobilize leaders. Your struggle with them may affect your sleep, keep you from eating, and depress you about what might happen. When fear of how people will react to your decision controls the decision, bad fear is in charge.

Remember, fear is an old problem and a common problem. For centuries, some of God's best people have struggled with fear. Leaders are not immune to fear. They learn to manage their fears and move forward anyway. Here are some biblical strategies for confronting fear and leading in spite of your fears.

Strategies for Overcoming Fear

There are seven biblical strategies for overcoming fear. Stated another way, these are strategies for developing courage. While the first one is foundational, the other six are not sequential. They are, instead, strategies you can continually use to confront and overcome your fears as a leader.

1. Be saved. Salvation in Jesus Christ is foundational to overcoming fear. In a broader context about salvation, Romans 8:15 says, "For you did not receive a spirit of slavery to fall back into fear." Your salvation experience with Jesus breaks the power of sin in your life. Sin is still very much a force in our world, but it no longer has control of you as a believer or as a leader. Apart from this spiritual relationship and its liberating results, you have no hope for facing down your fears.

Because of your salvation in Jesus Christ, you can face your fears and lead when you still feel afraid. All strategies emerge from this relationship. Without this relationship, every other strategy is a dead work of the flesh. Handling fear is a spiritual battle, not a psychological ploy. Facing fear is a spiritual reality, often fought on the battlefield of your mind.

Romans 8:15 continues: "but you received the Spirit of adoption, by whom we cry out, 'Abba, Father!'" Some relationships have special privileges. As a Christian, you can cry out to your Father because you enjoy a unique relationship with him. You are his child—his son or daughter. My children have certain privileges that come from their relationship with me. They can call me any time, day or night, and have my help with any problem. They can access my resources and will someday receive an inheritance. Relationships have privileges.

Your relationship with God as Father through your salvation in Jesus brings spiritual privileges you enjoy as his child. Your bondage to fear was broken when you became a Christian. Fear was not broken, but its control over you was. Your salvation enables you to implement the other six strategies in this section.

2. Practice God's presence. God is your Father. Better than any earthly father, he is always with you. Learning to live this reality is not a psychological trick; it's a spiritual reality. The psalmist wrote "The LORD is with me; I will not be afraid. What can man do to me?" (Ps. 118:6 NIV).

This simple affirmation, "God is with me; I will not be afraid" is a powerful resource to remind a leader he or she is not alone. There is something very comforting about companionship, about knowing we are not alone in a difficult situation. When my oldest son was about four, we went to a church building late one Saturday night. All the lights were off. We entered the auditorium on the opposite side from the light switches and were quietly shuffling our way through the dark. His little hand felt its way into my hand—and it sure felt good! While my son was reaching out in the dark for his dad, I was just glad to have *anyone* with me. Dark church buildings can be scary places.

Sometimes, well-lit church buildings can also be scary places. Some worship services demand prophetic preaching, committee meetings require hard decisions, counseling sessions call for tough love, board meetings deal with controversial issues, and staff meetings can feel like combat zones. In every one of these situations, leaders feel fear but must lead anyway.

Leading while afraid is possible when you remember that God is with you. He is with you when you preach, when you lead a difficult meeting, when you

referee relational conflicts, when you make controversial decisions, and when you face competing agendas. God is with you. One of my favorite prayers
underscores the reality of God's presence with me
as a leader. It's a short, simple prayer, "Father, here
we go."

The emphasis is on "we." I pray this prayer
before I stand up to preach. I have often stopped
outside a meeting room, with my hand on the
doorknob, and prayed, "Father, here we go." I
pray this prayer before entering almost any difficult situation. I do not ask him to accompany
me; he *is always* with me. This prayer changes my
perspective, puts my fears in their place, and gives
me confidence that I am not alone. Military men
go into battle with the buddy system—partners
who watch each other's back and commit to bringing each other home alive. What a great picture of
God's presence—the ultimate buddy system for
Christian leaders.

3. Confront fear with truth. "You will know the
truth, and the truth will set you free" (John 8:32) is
oft quoted and applied in many situations. Does it
apply to confronting fear? Absolutely. John often
combined the themes of truth and light (for example, John 12:35–36), building on the Old Testament
use of these images. In Psalms, for example, walking
in the light (truth) is connected to overcoming fear
when the psalmist wrote, "The LORD is my light

and my salvation," and then asks, "Whom should I fear?" (Ps. 27:1).

The answer to this rhetorical question is "No one!" God provides light—truth—for us to walk in, and doing so overcomes fear. So many fears are irrational or caused by imaginary enemies, situations, or possible results. The *What if* monster roams the mind of every leader creating various scenarios of what might happen. *What if* people become angry with me, our ministry is hurt by my decision, we are making a huge mistake, it costs more money than we planned (it always does, by the way), the project takes longer than we thought, a personnel decision does not work out, and on and on and on.

Fear paralyzes leaders with questions about what *might* happen. Leaders are responsible to consider options, imagine possible outcomes, and manage strategies that may need to be adjusted on the fly. That's what leaders do. But stewing inwardly, having your gut in a knot all the time about what might happen, is not effective contingency management. Fear has the upper hand when that is a leader's experience.

Confronting fear with truth can be done in two ways. First, confront fear with biblical truth. Memorize key verses (like some in this chapter) that underscore what the Bible says about fear. Memorize passages that remind you of the core spiritual resources you have in your relationship with God. Meditate on the truth in these passages to change your thinking about fear.

Second, confront fear with what is true about your situation. Too often, our minds race through wild scenarios about what might happen and how bad it will be. When that happens, you need a reality check. What is the worst that could happen? You could lose your job. And then you would get another one. You could lose some friends. And then you would make new ones. You might die! But then you would be in heaven. This is not to make light of the painful, difficult results from some decisions a ministry leader has to make. But it does put our losses in perspective. The reality of what we imagine might happen to us is generally not as bad as what does happen to us.

4. Pray . . . hard! While my short prayer, "Father, here we go," is helpful on the spot—more prayer is needed to overcome the stronghold of fear. "I sought the LORD, and He answered me and delivered me from all my fears" is one leader's impassioned testimony (Ps. 34:4). Sometimes, fearful situations are ongoing. They test us over a prolonged period of time. The fear monster, seemingly slain, rears itself time and again.

One young man's struggle to enter ministry illustrates prayer as a strategy to overcome fear. He had many fears about the ministry based on his observations of ministry leaders, particularly his father who had been through many unfortunate ministry conflicts as a leader. Every time he considered entering ministry, his fears of what might happen to him, to his family, and to his future short-circuited the decision. He had to pray through his fears.

It took months, but he finally committed himself to ministry and now serves effectively. His fears were deeply rooted in his experiences as a child watching his father deal with negative situations. A significant breakthrough came when he realized that his father, while he had suffered very unfair treatment, had not given up on the church or the ministry. My young friend realized he was allowing fear to control him. After months of prayer, he came to realize God's confidence that enabled him to answer the call to ministry. Through prayer, he gained the insight needed to confront his fears and move forward.

The psalmist "sought the LORD," which implies more than a casual prayer. The tone implies persistent praying. Sometimes, a short prayer produces the needed change. But more often, when it comes to overcoming fear, it takes longer to pray through. Cracking the stronghold of fear requires focused prayer, use of Scripture in prayer, careful meditation while praying, and discerning the Spirit's promptings about the causes and solutions to the fear-producing situation.

Making the decision to move across the country and plant a church was a prolonged fearful experience for me. The decision took months, accompanied by many days and nights bracketed by prayer. My fears were many—would the move harm my family, would it limit my future ministry opportunities, would the new church succeed (and what if it didn't?), would we survive financially, would my pregnant wife's health be negatively impacted, would we be able to adjust to a new culture, and would our extended families understand the decision?

Each time I prayed through one of these issues, another one seemed to come up! Just when I found God's confidence about our family, financial fears would arise. When those were resolved, fears about the church's success would emerge. Praying those to resolution gave some relief, and then fears about my wife's health came to the forefront. You get the idea! One fear after another reared its ugly head to try to convince me to stay in the safety of my secure pastorate in a comfortable church.

But God had a different plan for us. Through prayer, one by one the fears fell by the wayside. God gave us the courage to make the right decision. When we moved, not one fear we had imagined came true. Our family thrived, the church was successful, we adapted beautifully to the new culture, and my wife delivered a healthy baby boy!

Pray *through* your deepest, most persistent fears!

5. Take action in faith. Several biblical leaders, previously listed, were afraid or were told not to be afraid. The good news is you are in good company when you, as a leader, struggle with fear. One of the strategies these leaders demonstrate is taking action in faith *while you are still afraid.*

James 2:17 says, "faith, if it doesn't have works, is dead." Taking action in faith is required of leaders. You will never be free from all fear. You may confront it with truth, pray through it, celebrate God's presence, and still be afraid. Some fear only flees when a leader stares it down and takes action in spite of feeling afraid.

Ezra, the Old Testament prophet, dramatically illustrates this principle. Surrounded by enemies of his effort to restore the temple, Ezra led the people to resume the sacrificial worship system: "They set up the altar on its foundation and offered burnt offerings for the morning and evening on it to the LORD *even though they feared* the surrounding peoples" (Ezra 3:3). Sometimes, leaders must take action even though they are still afraid. Waiting until you are fear-free means you are unlikely to act boldly as a leader.

Courageous actions in the face of fear produce a remarkable result. Fear, like the bully it is, retreats! My first experience with this was learning to witness the gospel to people. I felt a lot of anxiety about speaking to others about Jesus. What if they asked a question I couldn't answer, became upset with me, rejected the Lord, what if, what if, what if?! Fear had me down for the count.

But a friend helped me through my fears. He told me my fears about witnessing were normal and probably would not abate. His counsel? Witness anyway and the fears would go away. He started taking me with him on evangelistic visits. Then, in spite of my fears, he had me share the gospel in some of the visits. After a few months, he moved away and left me to continue our outreach program. For years, I have been making regular evangelistic home visits as a church leader and witnessing the gospel in public settings. I still feel some anxiety about witnessing, but I share my faith anyway. Fear evaporates in the spiritual power of talking about Jesus.

The same thing happens in other fearful situations. Preparing to meet a critic, handle a difficult personnel problem, or attend a difficult meeting can be fear-inducing. Often, however, what we imagine might happen is far worse than what does happen. Do not be immobilized by fear. Move ahead purposefully. Trust God to make fear flee as you confidently take action by faith.

6. Enjoy God's love. We have a Scripture plaque in our bedroom, hung when we were first married and moved with us to every place we have called home. It says, "There is no fear in love; instead, perfect love drives out fear, because fear involves punishment" (1 John 4:18). The plaque reminds us that love drives away fear, including the fearful situations we face as a couple. Love overcomes fear, not only in marriage, but in other significant relationships.

Much we fear involves punishment. Fear is often rooted in performance or performance-related expectations. If you do not perform up to a certain standard, real or imagined, you fear you will be judged. God does not relate to you that way. God loves you; case closed!

So where does this kind of devilish thinking come from? The Evil One is determined to undermine you anyway he can. Since you have discovered God's love expressed through Christ, you would think you would never doubt his love for you. But that is not the case. As a Christian leader, you can still doubt God's love. You would never express it that bluntly, but you express it plainly by how you act.

You still work to prove your worth, strain to demonstrate your value, base your self-esteem on what others think or say about you, and measure your success by external achievements like buildings, budgets, or baptisms. When you do these things, you deny the love of God. God's love is about acceptance, security, rest, and a profound sense of worth because of his relationship to you.

A good word for this self-inflicted mental punishment is "condemnation." Many leaders are punished by fear through the condemnation they feel and struggle to overcome. Leaders who fear they can never do enough or never quite measure up are victims of the internal condemnation fear produces. These kind of condemning strongholds are the deep wounds that drive insecure leaders.

The solution is to enjoy God's love for you. *Enjoy* might not be a word you are comfortable using to describe how you experience God's love. We tend to think how unworthy we are, how gracious God is, and therefore how stingy we need to be with God's love. In other words, we like it but we need to use it in small doses so as not to exhaust the supply.

God's love is unlimited. Enjoy it. Revel in it. Drink deeply from the well. Let God's love immerse you. God's love is perfect, and perfect love—enjoyed thoroughly—will drive out fear. It really will. As you rest securely in God's love, condemnation ceases, self-punishment stops, and fear diminishes.

7. Obey God's laws. Moving from enjoying God's love to obeying God's laws may seem like an abrupt change of direction and perspective. Not really. God's laws, commands, and instructions are definitive expressions of his love. God knows what's good for you and tells you plainly. There is no guesswork with God on certain issues. He wants his people to be blessed and warns that certain behavior is too destructive to tolerate.

Both the Old and New Testaments have clear warnings about how fearful it is to disobey God.

God warns in Leviticus 26:15–16, "If you reject My statutes and despise My ordinances, and do not observe all My commands—and break My covenant, then I will do this to you: I will bring terror on you." Similar language is in Hebrews 10:26–27, "For if we deliberately sin after receiving the knowledge of the truth, there no longer remains a sacrifice for sins, but a terrifying expectation of judgment." Terror and terrifying expectation of judgment await the person who willfully disobeys God.

Many leaders struggle with fears that obedience cures. Obedient leaders do not fear getting a sexually transmitted disease because they maintain moral purity. Honest leaders do not fear being caught stealing. Why? Because they are not taking anything from anyone. Obedience in financial matters means you do not fear creditors taking your property because you live on your income and pay your bills. God has spoken clearly on many issues. When you obey him, you have much less to fret about or fear.

When you obey God's clear instructions, many common fears become irrelevant. Like a toothless tiger, these fears can growl but they have no bite. Your obedience renders some fearful situations completely powerless. Resolving some fears is just this simple. Obey God! Get under the protective covering of his Word on clearly "right or wrong" issues. When God gives clear directions, obey him and enjoy safety and absence of fear. Disobedience leads to terror and terrifying judgment. If you are willfully disobeying God, you should be afraid! Nothing will help you until you repent and obey him.

Taking a Courageous Stand

Leaders must overcome fear because of the many situations in ministry that require courage. Circumstances that require courage in ministry include making decisions, changing a paradigm, risking new ventures, preaching prophetically, and enduring public vulnerability. Any of these can be a daunting task. Often these circumstances come in pairs or clusters—meaning the need for courage is increased exponentially.

Making decisions is a key function of leaders. While that seems obvious, it is amazing how many leaders struggle to make decisions. Leaders know the daily pressure of analyzing situations and making the best decision possible. We often decide complex issues. We work with limited information, sometimes on a short timetable. We do not always know all the facts. We decide based on what we know. That's hard, especially when all the facts simply cannot be known given the time allotted for the decision.

Leaders often make "best guess" decisions. We work with deadlines, without the luxury of interminable delay. Leaders make the call—up or down, win or lose, right or wrong. Some decisions, fortunately, are routine with limited consequences. But some are more significant. Those require courage to put your judgment and reputation on the line, often in a public forum with very public consequences.

In rare or dramatic circumstances, a leader must take a courageous stand on an issue of incredible significance. One pastor took a significant stand when he discovered his church leaders were secretly involved in a white supremacy group. Another ministry leader lost his job when he publicized financial irregularities in his organization (which later collapsed from mismanagement). A deacon led his church to confront a popular pastor who was stealing church funds. A pastor dismissed a much-loved worship leader for involvement with pornography and then bore additional criticism when he insisted that the church support the young man through a recovery program.

Ministry leaders also take courageous stands on public issues. Taking stands on abortion, same-sex marriage, sex outside of marriage, homosexual behavior, and sex education programs in public schools are all part of ministry leadership these days.

One of the best examples of a courageous stand is the young men who found themselves in a fiery furnace (Dan. 3). King Nebuchadnezzar ordered everyone to bow down and worship a large statue of himself. Shadrach, Meshach, and Abednego refused. They were tossed into the fiery furnace, blazing so hot it killed the men who threw them in. God protected them and brought them out alive. That's the good news, the happy ending.

But when they went into the furnace they had no assurance they would come out. They did not take their stand because they knew they would be protected. They took it because they knew it was right. In fact, their explanation to the king was clear. "If the God we serve exists, then He can rescue us from the furnace of blazing fire, and He can rescue us from the power of you, the king. But *even if He does not rescue us,* we want you as king to know that we will not serve your gods or worship the gold statue you set up" (Dan. 3:17–18).

This story reveals several ingredients for a courageous stand. First, be sure you choose a worthy issue. Know the difference between a whim, preference, perspective, proverb, principle, conviction, and law. Second, be sure it matters. Asking, "Is this a hill you want to die on?" is a legitimate question. Not everything deserves a courageous stand. Compromise is not always a dirty word. Three, be responsible for your actions and their results. Courage acts no matter the consequences. Only fools expect to be bailed out. Fourth, be prepared to suffer. God never promises to bail out every leader who takes a stand. When Paul was jailed in Philippi, God sent an earthquake to save him (Acts 16:26). Later, however, he spent two years in jail waiting resolution of his case (Acts 24:27). God is not obligated to save you and does not always bail out courageous leaders. Sometimes, God allows leaders to suffer.

———◆———

Showing courage begins with confronting immobilizing fear. As you confront fear, facing it with the strategies outlined in this chapter, your courage will grow. As it grows, you can expect God to allow ever-greater tests for you. The longer you lead, the more challenging the situations God will allow you to face. Doing what is right may cost you. But, in those critical moments, do not let fear of what might happen keep you from doing the right thing.

While God often delivers, what if he doesn't and the worst happens? Then you can say with Paul, "To live is Christ and to die is gain" (Phil. 1:21 NIV). Heaven is the worst thing that can happen to you!

CHAPTER TEN

Sustaining Passion

EARLY IN MY first pastorate, I attended a ministers' luncheon and sat across from a veteran pastor. Others at the table welcomed me to the community and made typical small talk about their families and past ministry experiences. Then someone asked me to describe my vision for my church. Enthusiastically, I outlined the opportunities and challenges in our church and community. I shared my vision for how we could reach people, how we might need to enlarge our facilities or relocate, and how willing the church seemed to expand its ministry and grow.

I concluded by saying, "I am really excited about our future and the vision God has given me." The pastor across the table finally made his one and only comment, "You'll get over it."

His slumped shoulders and permanent scowl punctuated his comment. It was obvious that he had lost any enthusiasm or excitement about ministry. He was beaten and defeated. Whatever passion had prompted him to enter ministry was gone. As I left that luncheon, I prayed, "Lord, please don't ever let that happen to me."

So far, it has not. God has moved me, however, from excitement about the ministry to passion for ministry. There is a significant difference between excitement and passion. Excitement, like most feelings, ebbs and flows. But passion is deeper than a feeling. Passion is a sustaining force God ignites for ministry. Over the years, several principles about how God does this have become clear.

Passion Means Compassion

Passion is an interesting word. In modern usage, passion often has a positive connotation. But in the New Testament, the word most often translated passion usually has a more negative meaning. It is usually associated with baser passions, such as lust or evil desires. The New Testament word more closely tied to the modern notion of passion is *compassion*.

The word translated *compassion* literally means "rumbling in the gut or stirring of the bowels." That is not too appealing until you remember that the bowels, not the heart, were the symbolic center of life in the first-century worldview. Compassion, in the biblical sense, is the deep motive that drives a person's actions. Compassion is part of a person's core values, the heart issues that propel actions. This contrasts with the modern view of compassion that is generally more of an emotional response to painful or unfortunate circumstances.

Every leader needs to be empathetic in situations that demand caring ministry. Genuinely identifying with and supporting followers emotionally is part of leading them. This is what is typically meant by compassion today. While this is important, it is not the same as having sustained passion for ministry. Every leader must discover ways to sustain passion. Remember, the biblical idea of compassion (not the modern notion) closely approximates this concept of passion. These following concepts, based on the New Testament understanding of compassion, will help you understand how to sustain passion for ministry.

The Best Model

Jesus is the best model for compassion, or sustaining passion, for ministry. Matthew 9:35–36 records that Jesus "felt compassion for them." This phrase is tucked within a summary statement of Jesus' recent ministry. The summary helps us understand what it takes to sustain passion for ministry.

Jesus really connected with people. Matthew wrote, "Jesus went to all the towns and villages, teaching in their synagogues, preaching the good news of the kingdom, and healing every disease and every sickness." In short, Jesus spent a lot of time with people.

The Bible often has summary statements that can be read quickly but encompass days, weeks, or even months of ministry. Jesus "went to all the towns and villages." Have you ever considered how much time was involved? Jesus walked, or rode a slowly walking animal, everywhere he went. His available modes of transportation did not allow Jesus to rush through the towns and villages. He went slowly. He identified with them where they lived, worked, and worshipped. He was among them and really *with* them.

Jesus spent time teaching and preaching. Those two activities take time. Jesus also spent time healing. With rare exception, Jesus touched the people he healed. Jesus connected with people. He took time with people. Jesus knew people and ministered to them personally and individually.

Jesus saw people as they really are. Matthew continued, "When He [Jesus] saw the crowds, He felt compassion for them because they were weary and worn out, like sheep without a shepherd." Jesus saw people as they really were, not as they appeared to be or as they may have tried to be. Jesus saw more than faceless crowds. He saw individuals who were weary and worn out, helpless and hurting.

The stories in the chapter preceding this summary passage record Jesus ministering to individuals.

Jesus healed a paralytic, called a disciple, confronted the Pharisees and John's disciples, healed a woman, resuscitated a young girl, restored sight to a blind man, and cast a demon out of a man. Jesus saw the crowd as a collection of individuals with specific needs requiring personal ministry. Jesus could have said, "Everybody is cured, confronted, or delivered," and it would have been done. But he did not. He worked with people personally.

Sustaining passion in ministry is rooted in the ability to see people as they really are. Doing so changes your perspective. My oldest son, as a younger teenager, taught me this lesson with a profound statement. We were discussing the morality of nude dancing. He had some reasons, borrowed from his buddies, why viewing nude dancers was acceptable.

After listening to his flawed reasoning, I was ready to shoot down all his arguments. There are many reasons voyeurism is harmful. But a check in my spirit stopped me from turning our conversation into a point-by-point debate. Instead, I lowered my voice and said, "Son, we can't watch nude dancers because each woman is someone's daughter, someone's sister. They aren't objects of lust; they're real people." He thought about it a few seconds and replied, "You're right, Dad. *Everything changes when you see people for who they really are.*"

Exactly! When you see people as a mass of sinners, a crowd who exists to drain you, needy people who will never amount to anything, or church members who exist to support you, you will not treat them compassionately or have sustaining passion to serve them. But when you see people as they really are, passion stirs deep within you. How can you, indwelled by the Spirit of Jesus, respond any other way?

Embracing People, Sustaining Passion

Connecting with people and seeing them as they really are is essential for sustaining passion. When you meet a radical feminist protestor, do you see a political zealot or an angry, possibly abused woman with deep emotional needs? When you see a businessman neglecting his family to pursue wealth, do you think, *How dumb can he be?,* or do you think, *What makes him so insecure?* When a tattooed or pierced teenager passes you on the street, do you feel scorn for wasted potential or pain for someone desperately looking for acceptance and community?

Listing persons in these categories does not imply all their motives are impure or their actions are wrong. The point is not to create rigid categories but to challenge your impressions. Do you automatically judge people who are different from you and assume the worst? If you do, you are draining passion from your ministry. Seeing people who are different from you as Jesus might see them infuses you with passion for them.

Changing how you see people is vital for sustaining passion for ministry. Here is a model for changing your perspective, for changing the way you perceive the crowd around you. Here is some help for seeing people as Jesus sees them.

Accept People as They Are

This is a basic, yet often neglected, discipline for leaders. We often expect people to be more than they are and become angry when they disappoint us. We relate to people as we wish them to be, not as they really are. We expect too much from people. When you do this, you will always be disappointed.

Christian leaders are people developers. We want people to grow, improve, and change. And they do! But that does not change the fact that they have baggage. They grow in fits and spurts, not in a smooth way you can chart and measure. We also sometimes become frustrated when people act out their sinfulness. We forget that people really are sinners and will naturally act like it.

People have different levels of intelligence, giftedness, commitment, and potential. In spite of our "brilliant" leadership, every follower will not excel in every area of life. If you think they will, you are living in a dream world! Prepare to be disappointed and disillusioned. Your perspective on Christians prior to failure will largely determine how you respond to them when they fail. Did you have them on a pedestal, or did you more realistically see them as saved, yet still flawed, sinners?

One teenage girl attended a youth retreat about sexual purity. For two days, she learned about moral purity and how to resist sexual pressure and temptation. She returned home after making a serious, well-intentioned commitment to maintain her moral values.

A few months later she became pregnant. She was devastated. When she told me about the pregnancy, she apologized for "letting me down." It would have been easy to allow my disappointment to become the issue. She had ignored my instruction, embarrassed our church, and created problems in our youth ministry. She had lost so much—her virginity, her future plans, the respect of her parents, her relationships with her friends, and the high school experiences she would miss. My emotional response, however, was not the issue. The real problem was her pregnancy and helping her move forward the best way possible. Her behavior did not determine my pastoral effectiveness. It was important to keep that in perspective.

This principle will also give you sustaining passion for evangelizing people. For years, my hobby has been umpiring baseball. My umpire friends have been my primary community for evangelism and ministry. What is your impression when you see an umpire? a legalist? a hard-nosed, argumentative boor? a control freak? all of the above? Some umpires fit this stereotype (thankfully, most don't). Those that do are the men and women I most like to befriend.

It's easy to be put off by the profane language, arrogance, and bravado. But I am not easily distracted by the smoke screen. I see my umpire friends for who they really are. I see through the tough-guy façade to the brokenness. I see the damaged marriages, drinking problems, chain-smoking to relieve stress, and bawdy jokes to mask their fear of intimate relationships. I see them for who they really are, which invigorates passion for reaching them with the gospel. I am not disappointed when they act out their sinfulness. I expect it and accept them as they are.

It is reprehensible for any Christian leader to expect discipled behavior from the unconverted. Develop the spiritual and emotional discipline of accepting people as they are. Accept the good in people, but expect the bad to occasionally emerge. Most people are doing life as well as they can. No one wakes up and asks, "How can I be stupid today? What can I do to wreck my life?" Accept people as they are, not as you wish them to be or hope they will become.

Relate to People on Their Terms

A second part of embracing people is relating to them on their terms, on their turf. Jesus modeled this by going to homes, synagogues, and other public places. Leaders who want to develop passion for people must take the plunge! Leave the ivory tower of isolated Christian leadership and get out with people. No leaders can effectively lead people from their offices, no matter how technologically advanced they are. Turn off your computer and get with people!

One pastor schedules two hours of pastoral or evangelistic visitation every Saturday morning to get his heart right about the people he will preach to on Sunday. Going into homes and seeing how people really live, listening to them, and observing their families does something remarkable for him. It reminds him how people are really living, not how he imagines or wishes they were.

But home visitation is not the only way to do this. Several years ago I was the guest speaker at a women's Bible study at a country club. This interdenominational group had been together for about a year. They had been working through the book of Acts and had a list of questions they wanted to ask. A woman from my church who was part of the group arranged for me to meet with them. The questions were technical, challenging, and sent me back to my commentaries!

Over time, this relationship developed into a once-a-month question-and-answer session. When Christmas came, they invited me to their party that included their husbands. Most of these men were not Christians. They were driven businessmen with little evident spiritual interest. The ladies were concerned I might be offended because their husbands would be drinking at the party.

What would you do? For me, it was an easy decision. I went to the party. I met the men on their turf, on their terms. Meeting them, getting to know them, and discerning the issues keeping them from committing themselves to Jesus kindled my passion for these men. Within a few months, the first of them became a Christian.

What would have happened if a leader had not been willing to meet them on their terms, on their turf? Eternal consequences! Until I met these men, they were anonymous. After I met them, they became people I cared deeply about. I was compelled to reach them for Jesus. Passion is generated and sustained by getting out where people are, getting to know them, and experiencing life from their perspective.

Meet the Needs of People

A third way to kindle passion for people is to discover their needs and meet them. Some leaders debate the difference between real needs and felt needs. There is a difference—but only to the leader! To the person with the need, the felt need is the real need. Discovering needs is not that difficult. Making the sacrifice to meet them is the difficult part.

A few years ago, I joined the board of a youth sports organization. I really wanted to develop a ministry relationship with the president of the board, so I started being alert to his needs and meeting them. Some of his needs, those related to his responsibilities, were obvious. But I constantly looked for ways to serve him personally.

After two years of trying to build our friendship, his mother died. His wife told me three weeks later, "We almost called you to do a service for her." That was a missed opportunity. Disappointed but undeterred, I kept looking for ways to serve him. Two years later, his father died. This time he called! I officiated a service for his father and further cemented our relationship.

Two more years passed. More needs were met, both personal and related to our board service. Then, a major marriage problem arose. He called and said, "Jeff, today I really need a friend." Within minutes I was at his house and the door was finally opened for real ministry. For about six years I had been serving him in practical ways, all the time hoping for a breakthrough to a deeper level of ministry. Finally, it happened.

Passion for this man and his family was generated by the investment I made in him. When you put six years of ministry into a person, you will develop strong feelings for him or her.

Serve People with Abandon

Finally, sustaining passion comes when you release yourself to really embrace the people you are responsible to lead. Some leaders keep one eye on the horizon, always looking for greener pastures. One pastor seemed to be talking continually to some search committee. The thrill of being pursued apparently met some deep need. I often wondered if that need would have been met more meaningfully if he had closed off all options and really given himself emotionally to the church he was serving. I think it would have.

When my wife and I got married, we vowed to never even mention the word *divorce.* We had some difficult years early in our marriage (who doesn't?). But the fact we had no other option forced us to learn to live happily with one another. We were driven to solve our conflicts and build our marriage. When you completely commit yourself to a relationship, something deep happens. You find yourself emotionally attached to people at a depth you cannot explain. That is passion you are feeling. Passion grows in the greenhouse of total commitment.

In my first pastorate, we celebrated come-and-go Lord's Supper services on Christmas Eve. A different deacon served the Supper on the hour from late afternoon through the evening. I would often sit in the back of the dimly lit sanctuary and watch the drama of church members observing the Lord's Supper with a small group of fellow believers, served by a trusted friend. It was a poignant scene.

Sitting there, the memories of the previous year of ministry would flood my mind. New converts having their first Christian Christmas, families saved through ministries of our church, teenagers newly committed to missions or ministry, recent widows and widowers, and pregnant women expecting their first child all reminded me of how privileged I was to be a pastor. What a wonderful gift from God to be shepherd of part of his flock!

If you want deeper passion for people, commit yourself to them and serve them with reckless abandon. Stop watching the clock and counting the cost! Emotionally, give yourself to them entirely. Stop holding back and looking around for a better deal! Spiritually, sacrifice your future dreams on the altar of your present responsibility. Commit yourself to be fully engaged with those you are responsible to lead. When you do, passion will well up from deep within.

As you consider these strategies for embracing the people you lead and developing sustaining passion for ministry, an acrostic emerges.

*A*ccept people as they are.
*R*elate to people on their terms.
*M*eet the needs of people.
*S*erve people with abandon.

Put your ARMS around people. Embrace them. Let them get into your heart. Develop an emotional attachment to your followers. Christian leadership is not primarily a professional responsibility. It is a professional *relationship*.

Time Out to Rest

Wait a minute, you may be thinking. *People don't renew my passion. They drain me!* Me too! So, how can embracing people lead to sustaining passion? It happens when immersing yourself in relationships is balanced with another source of passion modeled by Jesus. That source is intentional rest.

Jesus not only modeled being with people; he also modeled getting away from people. Throughout the Gospels, Jesus modeled the principle of intentional rest. He went on prayer retreats—some private, and others with his closest friends. He went to parties, celebrations, and worship services. Jesus knew the importance of being alone, of being with friends, and of balancing the demands of ministry with rejuvenation through rest.

Many leaders are deluded by their own importance. They have, to quote a friend, "delusions of adequacy and illusions of indispensability." Are you like that? If you are, you probably have not developed the discipline of pulling away from your ministry responsibilities and resting. Finding the proper balance between embracing people and retreating regularly from the intensity of those relationships sustains passion. Jesus did it and you can too.

Rest Weekly

God laid down the law—work six days, rest one. Following this pattern sustains a person over the long haul. Leaders, because they are typically driven and energetic, often act like they are exempt from this principle. You are not exempt, no matter what!

Why is it so hard for Christian leaders to follow this simple pattern—work six days, rest one? Leaders have unpredictable and uneven work patterns. There is no normal workweek. Leaders are often people-pleasers. This makes them too willing to respond to every request for their time. Most leaders like their work and find it hard not to overcommit. Ministry is fulfilling and often fun! On the downside, some leaders have real emotional or psychological needs they try to satisfy through work. These leaders are workaholics and need help to break their addiction.

For most of us, the answer is to make a disciplined choice to simply say no to working seven days a week. This requires commitment to an intentional plan. For more than twenty years, I have rested one day a week from ministry responsibilities. Making this decision was difficult. I had some workaholic issues and also some other reasons for being so driven. But my wife and church leaders insisted we establish a regular schedule that included one "day off" per week.

How did we do it, and how have we maintained it? As a couple, we simply decided and did it. For many years, it was Thursday. Then, as our children grew older, we switched to Saturday. Later, when I changed from pastoral ministry to a leadership role that required weekend travel, we changed to Friday. For more than twenty years, we have managed to set aside one day per week to rest, refocus, and reset.

We have not been perfect or legalistic about this practice. We only rest one day per week, on average about forty-five weeks per year. Like all ministry leaders, sometimes our schedule simply has to accommodate events that conflict with our rest day. Emergencies happen, special events require special scheduling, and travel demands sometimes change schedules unexpectedly. But, look at it another way. For about forty-five weeks every year for more than twenty years we have had one day per week without any phone calls, any sermon preparation, any counseling appointments, any visits, any staff meetings, any cranky people to manage, or any e-mail to answer!

If you have not established this pattern, try these suggestions. Develop an annual ministry calendar and simply block out one day (the same day each week works best) per week. Block it out! No exceptions (although some will inevitably arise as the year unfolds). On that day, turn off your cell phone and do not check your e-mail. Do not go by the office. Let an answering machine screen your calls at home. If you have a secretary or staff, tell them not to call you except for real emergencies. And, teach them what a real emergency is! A broken water pipe in the church basement is not an emergency requiring your attention; the death of a church member is. If you live too close to your church, mission, or office, you may need to actually get away from your home for the day.

Do not be legalistic about what you can or cannot do on your rest day. The only thing you cannot do is work at ministry. We sometimes do nothing, go shopping, go to a movie, eat out for lunch, read all day, work on some crafts, fix up our house, or anything else we enjoy. The purpose of a weekly day of rest is not inactivity but a change of pace and emotional disengagement from the pressures of work.

Retreat Occasionally

Leaders need to pull away occasionally for more than one day. They need a multiday retreat to really renew themselves. This can take any number of forms, some of which involve work or preparation for future work.

Personal retreats include prayer retreats, going to a conference or meeting alone, marriage retreats (as a couple or with a group), and study retreats. Some leaders go away alone to plan a year of preaching or develop some significant strategy for their church or organization. All of these personal retreats can be restful.

Group retreats might include prayer retreats, staff retreats, attending a conference or meeting with a group of church leaders, or perhaps a camp or cruise with peers who share your level of responsibility in other churches or organizations.

All these experiences can be significant. Too often leaders measure what they "get out of" these kind of events by how thick the notebook they bring home. Learning new concepts is helpful, but disengaging from the daily grind and getting a fresh perspective is often the more important outcome.

Vacation Annually

Henry Ford casually asked potential executives he was interviewing to tell him about their vacation the previous year. The driven answer of "not being able to get away" because of "my commitment to the company" was the wrong answer. He felt anyone who was not able to plan his work so he could accomplish it in fifty weeks each year, rather than fifty-two, was not capable of managing a section of Ford Motor Company. Not taking appropriate vacation was a disqualifying offense.

Oh, that it were so for all ministry leaders! Leaders often have two or more weeks of paid annual vacation, and they leave it on the table. What a waste! Vacation rest is a wonderful privilege and a tremendous opportunity to rest, reconnect with family, and rejuvenate for future work demands.

But do not make the mistake common to American culture. Vacation is often defined as "covering as much ground and spending as much money as possible." Neither will leave you rested. Some travel can be fun, but conquering ground and going into debt creates stress rather than relieves it.

When our children lived at home, we developed a pattern that worked well for us. We took some vacation around the Christmas holidays and simply stayed home. We turned off the cell phone and e-mail and enjoyed family time. We did traditional

Christmas events (such as driving around looking at Christmas lights, which my children loathed). We spent very little money and had maximum family time together.

Then, once a year, we took some kind of family trip. These were not always elaborate trips. Some years, depending on resources, they were very simple. The issue was not distance from home but emotional and intellectual distance from work. This pattern worked well for our family. We traveled some, had neat adventures, and saw some national treasures. We also had extra family time around an important holiday. Now, as our adult children establish their lives, we are developing new models of how we will do vacation rest.

Vacation rest is helpful when it restores you, strengthens your family, and you return ready to get back to work. If you come back and need a vacation to recover from your vacation, something is probably not working with your plan. Make adjustments and capitalize on the opportunity and privilege of vacation rest to make you a more effective leader.

—◆—

Sustaining passion for ministry is possible. Do not be like the pastor who tried to quench my vision. Embrace people. Deepen your ministry relationships. Abandon yourself emotionally to the people you serve. Ask God to give you fresh eyes to see people for who they really are.

And then, from time to time, pull completely away from everyone and rest. Learn both disciplines—immersion in the lives of people and retreating from ministry relationships—to retool for future ministry. This is not a contradiction; it is a healthy cycle that leads to emotional health, indefatigable commitment, and deep passion that will sustain your ministry over a lifetime.

CHAPTER ELEVEN

Continuing the Quest for Character

THIS BOOK ENDS with a comma, not a period. The quest for character is a continuing pursuit. No leader can ever claim to be exactly like Jesus. To do so would be arrogant, thus disproving the point. You are on a journey toward Christlikeness that will not end until you meet Jesus face-to-face. Then, finally, "we will all be changed" (1 Cor. 15:51).

Until then, keep character development your priority. Our world is too busy and moves too fast for much meditative reflection. We are pushed to "do" not to "be." Leaders are expected to make things happen, and we do! But wise leaders view their roles from God's perspective. Wise leaders remember that God's first objective is working in us to form the image of Jesus. He does this while simultaneously working through us to expand his kingdom. Only a magnificent, omniscient Father could accomplish both compatible purposes so beautifully.

An Audience of One

The challenge, in the midst of so many competing agendas and expectations, is to focus on the priority of your relationship with God. Paul faced this problem as an early church leader. The Corinthian church had a problem with factions created by members placing too much emphasis on celebrity leaders (1 Cor. 3:1–7). Paul pointedly wrote, "It is of little importance that I should be evaluated by you or by a human court. In fact, I don't even evaluate myself. For I am not conscious of anything against myself, but I am not justified by this. The One who evaluates me is the Lord" (1 Cor. 4:3–4).

Paul identified three categories of evaluators leaders often struggle to please. First, he placed little stock in how church members evaluated him ("you" referring to the Corinthian Christians). Second, he placed the same limited value on public opinion ("a human court" referring to public proceedings). Finally, he refused to trust self-evaluation ("myself"), even when it seemed positive or at least neutral ("not conscious of anything").

These same three kinds of evaluators are still a struggle for most Christian leaders. We worry about what church members think of us. Their response to our leadership makes a difference in many areas—from the growth of the church to the size of our paycheck. Public opinion matters to us. We do not want to be criticized by community leaders or unfairly characterized in the media. As one leader said, "You know it's going to be a bad day when *60 Minutes* is waiting in your office when you arrive."

Leaders also struggle with honest self-appraisal. We are usually too hard on ourselves when things are rough. We compound that by deflecting credit when things go well. Most leaders are reluctant to celebrate their strengths for fear of drifting toward self-absorption or self-promotion. Occasionally, some leaders become arrogant, puffed up by their pride of position or accomplishment. Frankly, this does not happen too often. Most Christian leaders are well aware of their frailty and sinfulness. Most Christian leaders err too often toward self-condemnation rather than self-celebration.

All three categories of people—church members, community, and self—are inadequate evaluators. Paul concluded, "The One who evaluates me is the Lord." That must be our conclusion as well. We must determine to live for an audience of One. Doing so will liberate us from the treadmill of doing leadership and free us to be leaders. Limiting your focus to what God thinks of you will set you free from the tyranny of external expectations.

All leaders have followers with multiple expectations, agendas, and needs. These cannot be ignored. Some of them are appropriate. After all, leaders are responsible *to lead.* Narrowing your focus to please an audience of one does not liberate you from external expectations. It frees you from the *tyranny* of what others want from you.

The issue is control. Will you be controlled by what others want from you or by what God is doing in you? Will you focus on doing things for God or on allowing God to do things in you? Will you measure success by the organization you build or the character shaped within you?

Balance is important. Leaders serve people, serve God, and build organizations. Without question, we must do these things. Shirking responsibility is never acceptable for a true leader. The crucial point is leadership activities are not the ultimate measure of God's leader-shaping work. Your ultimate focus must be on God's purpose to shape the character of Jesus Christ in you.

Usually, acknowledging God as our Ultimate Evaluator concludes with an admonition (or at least an attitude) that says, "Get it right or God will get you." That is not Paul's message, nor should it be our expectation. Concluding this section on being judged by God, he wrote, "And then praise will come to each one from God" (1 Cor. 4:5).

Do you believe that? When the final curtain falls and your life as a Christian leader is evaluated, do you expect to be condemned or congratulated? Most expect to be condemned. Being held accountable for our actions, however, does not equal blanket condemnation. It also means God notices our growth in Christ and the good things we have done for his kingdom. Those will be celebrated! Praise *will come* to you, from God, for who you were and what you accomplished for him.

What's Next for Me?

More growth into the image of Jesus! While writing this book, two new issues arose that reveal inadequacy in my character. Both will require intentional effort on my part to change. The first deficiency needs to be fixed immediately by changing a habit to create new discipline. Solving the second problem will be a long-term process. God has allowed circumstances forcing me to grow in new ways. My first reaction was to complain, whining for several days to the Father (and my coworkers) about how unfair life is. But the Joseph Principle came to mind, and I realize God is once again allowing circumstances out of my control to force me to grow.

What's Next for You?

The next step for you is creating a personal action plan for shaping character. You should create that plan while anticipating success. God is already at work to create the image of Christ in you. Why would you expect this process to fail? Why would you expect it to be onerous? God is your ally and will reward you richly for who you become in Christ and what you do for his kingdom.

Each chapter in this book has included specific steps or strategies to help develop character. Select the most pressing issues and create strategies to facilitate change. These are choices that, over time, will make a tremendous difference. Remember, character is not shaped quickly. Habits do not change overnight. Be patient, but persistent, as you move forward.

Choose one or two areas to work on first. Perhaps you need to improve discipline or be more courageous. Moral purity or servanthood may be your pressing issues. You may be thinking, *I need to work on all these qualities.* Caution: attacking on all fronts will leave you feeling overwhelmed. Choose one area and focus on it for awhile. Then choose a different area. Plan to keep at this process for years, not months or days.

Remember, all this takes time. These principles and practices have taken about twenty years to develop. Most of them have been learned, as you have read, the hard way. Trying to copy everything written here, like some checklist on steroids, is impossible. Doing that will frustrate you! Blindly doing certain practices, reducing this process to working a formula for leadership development, also misses the point. Some of my experiences will not help you, no matter how carefully you replicate them. Rather than simply copying my experience, ask God for fresh application of these principles to pertinent practices for you.

Finally, stay alert to how God is continually working to shape your character. He is working through his Word and your circumstances. He is working through events you cannot control. He will also work through projects and practices you structure for character development. Practice disciplined discernment to discover the depths of insight God wants you to have about yourself, life, and ministry.

Shaping the image of Jesus in you will be a life-long process. God may seem slow, but he is sure. He is relentless in his pursuit of the image of Jesus in his children. Cooperating with God is a surefire way to simplify your life and enjoy the process.

Being remade in the image of Jesus never ends! So, taking the next step means _____

_____

_____

_____

_____

_____

_____

_____

_____